ENERGIZING
INDIA

ENERGIZING INDIA

Fuelling a Billion Lives

EDITED BY
SHREERUPA MITRA

Published by
Rupa Publications India Pvt. Ltd in association with
The Energy Forum 2019
7/16, Ansari Road, Daryaganj
New Delhi 110002

Sales Centres:
Allahabad Bengaluru Chennai
Hyderabad Jaipur Kathmandu
Kolkata Mumbai

Copyright © The Energy Forum, 2019

The views and opinions expressed in this book are
the authors' own and the facts are as reported by them which have been verified to
the extent possible, and the publishers and The Energy Forum are not in any way
liable for the same.

All rights reserved.
No part of this publication may be reproduced, transmitted,
or stored in a retrieval system, in any form or by any means,
electronic, mechanical, photocopying, recording or otherwise,
without the prior permission of the publisher.

ISBN: 978-93-5333-389-8

First impression 2019

10 9 8 7 6 5 4 2 3 1

The moral right of the authors have been asserted.

Printed in India

This book is sold subject to the condition that it shall not,
by way of trade or otherwise, be lent, resold, hired out, or otherwise circulated,
without the publisher's prior consent, in any form of binding or
cover other than that in which it is published.

CONTENTS

Foreword   *vii*
   Fatih Birol

Introduction   *xiii*
   Shreerupa Mitra

1. India's Quest for Economic Growth and Energy Security   1
   Daniel Yergin

2. India's Energy Challenge   13
   Anil Kakodkar

3. India Takes its Place of Prominence on the Energy Stage   29
   Mohammad Sanusi Barkindo

4. Household Energy Transition in India and Elsewhere: The Role of LPG   48
   Kirk R. Smith and Abhishek Jain

5. Journey towards a Gas-based Economy: Decarbonizing India for a Sustainable Future   73
   Dharmendra Pradhan

6. Reforms in the Oil and Gas Sector   94
   Adil Zainulbhai

7.	Coal in India's Economy: An Agenda for Reforms *Arvind Panagariya and Anil Jain*	118
8.	The Role of Renewable Energy in India's Journey towards a Low Carbon Future *Debasish Mishra*	136
9.	The Role of Sustainable Finance in Supporting a Green Energy Transition *Satya Sundar Tripathi*	156
10.	A New Paradigm in Energy Diplomacy *S. Jaishankar*	180
11.	India: The Dual Challenge and Energy Investment Opportunities *Bob Dudley*	196
12.	Powering the US–India Energy Relationship *Nisha Biswal*	207
13.	The 'Digital Operations' Imperative for the Oil, Gas and Chemicals Industry in India *Ashwin Jacob*	215
14.	Preparing India's Workforce for the Fourth Industrial Revolution *Subha Srinivasan and Kumar Kandaswami*	243

Contributors   267

FOREWORD

Fatih Birol

In 2017, India became an associate member of the International Energy Agency (IEA). The IEA is far richer for having India in the family, given India's importance in global energy markets and the remarkable insights it provides to other members. I have praised India's energy policy achievements around the world and highlighted the lessons other countries can learn. At present, India faces an unenviable challenge—building a secure and sustainable energy system to power its remarkable economic growth.

Globally, the energy system is in transition. Oil markets are entering a new period of volatility and uncertainty. Electricity is expected to have a more prominent role in the global energy system in the future while the declining costs of solar and wind technology put renewable energy at the forefront of the energy discourse for future generations. Meanwhile, the sustainability of the energy industry is becoming more important as greenhouse gas emissions are rising again, with cities continuing to struggle with the pollution generated from energy consumption and energy-intensive industries.

India is rapidly becoming one of the most important countries in the global energy system, while dealing with many of the challenges facing the global energy sector. Energy will continue to underpin India's rapid economic growth and human development, making India the largest source of energy demand growth in the coming decades. India's energy use doubled between 2000 and 2015. The IEA expects its demand to double yet again by 2040. This would bring India's energy demand to half that of China's in 2040, up from a third today.

India's remarkable progress in providing universal access to energy has been a contributor to this large demand growth. It has taken huge strides towards providing access to energy for chunks of its population while addressing environmental challenges of meeting this spike in energy demand. Since 2000, India has brought electricity to around half a billion people, and we expect that with the current programmes, an additional 250 million people could gain access to electricity in the next five to ten years—effectively achieving universal household access to electricity. Access to energy is critical for human development. It expands economic opportunities and is vital for providing a range of services, which improve living standards, health and education outcomes. In 2018, India announced that it had brought electricity to all of its villages, many of them getting access for the first time. The scale of this achievement is commendable.

India has also taken major steps to expand access to clean cooking fuel to more households (see Figure 1). The Ujjwala programme has brought Liquefied Petroleum Gas (LPG) for cooking to fifty million households in India, reducing their exposure to pollution from burning biomass—a major cause of respiratory diseases.

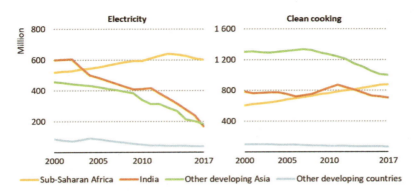

Figure 1: Population without modern energy access
Source: *World Energy Outlook 2018, IEA*

While the growth in energy demand over the past decade has mostly come from households and the services sector, the Indian government's policy of building India's manufacturing base means that the next phases of economic expansion are likely to be driven by a surge in energy-intensive industrial activity. The increased focus on manufacturing is likely to lead to energy demand growth from industry, outpacing the other sectors, such as domestic households and the services sector. This could push the total energy demand in 2040 to over four times the level in 2000.

The Indian Government has made progress in reducing the energy intensity of economic activities through innovative and ambitious energy efficiency measures. Over the past decade, the energy intensity of GDP in India has fallen by a quarter. Exemplifying the success of India's innovative approach, the state-owned Energy Efficiency Services Limited, through bulk procurements, has driven down the cost of LED bulbs in India to under $1 per bulb—an 80 per cent reduction since 2014. Consequently, 308 million bulbs have been replaced by LEDs. In

2017, 23 per cent of India's energy use was covered by mandatory energy efficiency policies and programmes, such as the Perform, Achieve and Trade scheme, which led to significant improvements in industrial energy efficiency. Programmes like these could reduce India's energy intensity by another one-third from today's level.

The Indian government is already taking steps to address the significant challenges posed by this growing demand for energy. Fossil fuels are likely to continue to dominate the supply of energy, engendering a host of environmental and economic considerations for the government. Air pollution is a serious health hazard for those living in India's major cities, as levels continuously exceed the safe limits laid down by the World Health Organization (WHO)—sometimes by an order of magnitude. The socio-economic impacts of this pollution are huge but could provide an impetus for reducing emissions from energy consumption. Further impetus for making adjustments in energy sources will come from the need to reduce global emissions of greenhouse gases.

In 2014, these considerations led to the announcement by India of achieving a renewable energy target of 175 GW by 2022. In 2017, India had a total installed capacity of 52 GW of solar and wind generation and 48 GW of hydro generation. Meeting the 2022 targets should set India on a path to increase renewable capacity by 8 per cent a year in the coming decades (see Figure 2). The ambitious roll-out of renewable generation will require significant investment and create challenges for an already burdened electricity network.

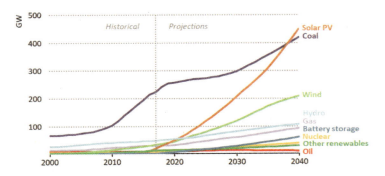

Figure 2: Installed capacities by source in India in the IEA New Policies Scenario
Source: *World Energy Outlook 2018, IEA*

Over the coming years, the Indian electricity market will change markedly to cope with the increased penetration of renewable generation and the huge growth in the reach and quality of the electricity network. Extending the reach of the network as well as coping with the increased volumes of electricity will require significant investment in transmission and distribution. Power markets and commercial structures will need to adapt to these changes in order to attract investment and to deal with the intermittency of renewable generation.

Even with the ambitious roll-out of renewable generation, coal continues to hold the largest share in total primary energy demand. India is both one of the largest coal producers and importers globally. Coal currently fuels around 75 per cent of power generation in India, and while its share may decrease, coal use in power generation is likely to continue to grow in absolute terms. Increasing domestic coal production will come with economic and logistical challenges—meaning coal imports are also likely to rise.

India's coal production is located far from many major demand centres. Therefore, a lot of production requires transporting across the country, further straining the rail system and increasing the cost of coal delivered to the plants. Also, India's domestic coal reserves are usually low grade, exacerbating the impact on the emission of pollutants and greenhouse gases—creating a greater need for higher quality imported coal. Furthermore, growth in coal demand is likely to outpace growth in domestic production, increasing the need for coal imports.

India continues to rely on imports of oil and gas, as domestic production struggles to match the rapid growth in demand. Reforms in the Indian oil production licensing regime, such as the Hydrocarbon Exploration and Licensing Policy (HELP), could help increase domestic production. However, the refining industry will continue to rely on imports for much of its demand. India's efforts to develop and expand its strategic petroleum reserves will provide a necessary buffer to the global markets, particularly when released strategically and in concert with global stockholdings. This will result in reducing India's vulnerability to the increasingly volatile oil and gas markets. Ultimately, securing a diverse range of suppliers of these key fuels will be critical to ensuring the security of supply across the energy sector in India.

A book such as this one, bringing together an impressive array of global energy experts, is invaluable in highlighting the various opportunities and challenges facing India—and many other countries—as they balance issues of energy security, reliability, pollution and greenhouse gas emissions. The plethora of perspectives on offer will no doubt inform, challenge and stimulate.

I would like to thank The Energy Forum for the opportunity to contribute to this compendium and trust that readers will find many useful insights.

INTRODUCTION

Shreerupa Mitra

Global energy systems define the material possibilities of our lives far more than what is acknowledged in the popular imagination. Lying as it does at the intersection of geopolitics, business and ethics, energy dynamics has ravaged and built civilizations, upended powerful regimes and consistently pushed the frontiers of what was known to be possible for the human race.

A good literature on energy, therefore, can never fall out of fashion.

The idea behind this book is to bring together the best minds from the world of energy, who analyze facets of energy dialectics at play. My team and I at The Energy Forum (TEF) have been fortunate to have had the opportunity to work with such stalwarts.

This book is an initiative of TEF—a think tank that explores issues around conventional and non-conventional sources of energy, researches technological advances and innovative business models in the sector and studies alternative approaches to powering 'last-mile' connectivity.

As an avid reader, I tend to resist a prescriptive linear pathway to completing a work of non-fiction. However, for those who do not share my affinity for chaos in literature, here is a basic thematic that should help negotiate this book. The first section has articles that give a general overview of the global energy landscape with emphasis on the Indian context. This comprises chapters by Daniel Yergin, Mohammad S. Barkindo and Anil Kakodkar. Chapters that dwell upon the reforms undertaken in the recent past follow the first thematic section. I have put the contributions of Kirk R. Smith and Abhishek Jain, Dharmendra Pradhan, Adil Zainulbhai, Arvind Panagariya and Anil Jain, Debasish Mishra, S. Jaishankar and Satya S. Tripathy under this category. The third section broadly deals with partnerships, with contributions by Bob Dudley and Nisha Biswal. The fourth part deals with digitalization and preparing for the Fourth Industrial Revolution (4IR) vis-à-vis the energy sector with writings from Ashwin Jacob and Shubha Srinivasan and Kumar Kandaswami. I have tapped into my editor's privilege to construct these broad categories—though, as we know, themes tend to seep into each other, especially when talking about something as vast and complex as the energy sector.

I would like to take this opportunity to thank all the contributors who took the time to write for us despite their heavy schedule. I have also had the solid support of family and friends without whom this book would not have been conceived or completed. In the interest of keeping this short, I will not name each one of them. You know who you are—my deep gratitude to you.

My hope is that readers will find this text to be a temporal capsule that captures the current unfolding of energy dynamics globally, and in India, and that it contains a touch of prescience that would nourish the shelf value of the writings.

January 2019

1

INDIA'S QUEST FOR ECONOMIC GROWTH AND ENERGY SECURITY

Daniel Yergin

INTRODUCTION

The equation is straightforward. Economic growth and increasing population equals rising energy consumption—and thus the need for more energy supplies. India knows this equation all too well. Its GDP has grown at an average rate of 7 per cent over the last five years. In the same period, its total energy consumption has increased at an annual rate of 4 per cent.

Overall, India is now well along on what the eminent economist Dr Vijay Kelkar has called the 'growth turnpike'. GDP could grow at 8 to 10 per cent annually in the years ahead—if supported with the right market-oriented policies and a steady world economy.

But movement up the growth turnpike—and achieving the $20 trillion economy—will be stalled without the energy supplies to fuel this growth. Assuring those supplies—and the right mix—is the great challenge for an India that needs to meet the needs of both rural and urban populations. The challenge is made even more demanding by the imperative to reduce air pollution and improve environmental conditions—both in the homes of rural Indians and in the sprawling cities of urban Indians—and meet climate objectives.

THE GLOBAL ENERGY SYSTEM TODAY—AND TOMORROW

Addressing India's energy needs raises three central questions: How to manage the nation's energy integration with global markets? How to develop its own oil and gas resources in a world competing for investment? And how to bring increasing amounts of renewable energy into the overall energy system?

These challenges come at a time when the global energy system itself is going through major changes. 'Energy transition' is the way these changes are described. This phrase has become a widely accepted and widely used refrain. Yet, there is little agreement as to what it means, or as to the speed at which it will unfold, or what the transition will look like two or three decades from now.

But the general elements are clear: global oil consumption will continue to grow but at a slower pace than in the past, natural gas will grow faster than oil, and liquefied natural gas (LNG) even faster. The fastest growth of all will be registered by wind and solar—what are called 'modern renewables', to distinguish them from the traditional polluting biomass fuels used in rural areas.

Three technologies have disrupted and changed the vectors for global energy. The shale revolution—born a decade and a half ago in the US—has shaken global oil and gas markets. During this period, the US has gone from importing 60 per cent of its oil to under 15 per cent. Instead of being a declining producer, it has now leapfrogged ahead of Russia and Saudi Arabia to become the world's number one producer. The old dichotomy of what had held for decades—Organization of the Petroleum Exporting Countries (OPEC) and non-OPEC nations—has given way to the new reality of the Big Three—the US, Russia and Saudi Arabia.

The US has also overtaken Russia to become the world's number one producer of natural gas. Unthinkable a few years ago, India now imports both oil and gas from the US, providing a whole new constructive dimension to the relationship between the two countries.

The other big change is in the two renewable technologies—the changing cost of solar and wind and their consequent rapid growth worldwide. In 2017, worldwide, more money was invested in solar and wind than in conventional fossil and nuclear power generation. The reasons for the growth are both on the supply- and demand-side.

On the supply side, the costs of both wind and solar have fallen significantly in the last decade. The decrease in solar is especially dramatic—an 80 per cent decline in the cost of panels. One major reason is the extensive overcapacity in the Chinese manufacturing goliath, which alone supplies about 70 per cent of global panels—an oversupply that has stimulated intense competition and price-cutting. Technological improvements in wind have made taller, better engineered towers possible that can more efficiently absorb the energy out of wind.

On the demand side, the driving forces are large scale and have led to extensive government policies around the world to support these technologies—incentives, subsidies and mandates. These emerge out of the dual concerns about local and regional pollution and global concerns about climate change and its potential impacts.

Renewables are the fastest growing source of power generation but still make up a very small proportion of the generation mix.

In its central forecast, the International Energy Agency (IEA) foresees modern renewables achieving 16 per cent of energy generation by 2040. In its more aggressive scenarios, renewables will reach 38 per cent of generation. In its scenarios for total energy in 2040, fossil fuel's share ranges from 60 per cent to 78 per cent—the latter hardly unchanged from today. So the potential growth in renewables can be considerable. Yet large-scale flows of intermittent and variable power—wind and solar-generated electricity—into electric grids pose significant challenges for grid management. At this point, despite hopes for the future, storage at scale does not exist for electricity. What seems likely is that natural gas generation will play an increasing role, paired with new renewables, to smooth out the intermittency and variability. In the US, the shares of both natural gas and renewables in power generation has grown rapidly at the expense of coal.

INDIA'S CHANGING ENERGY LANDSCAPE

How does India fit into the picture—both today and tomorrow? Today, India presents a contrast of a largely agrarian country with a dynamic, relatively modernized and non-industrial, non-agrarian services economy. This brings the requirement to supply rural areas, where most of the population live, and yet meet the demand for higher quality energy supply for a relatively smaller population base in cities and in the services and industrial sectors of the economy.

While seeking to satisfy both sets of demand, India is at the same time going through its own energy transition. Currently, the energy mix is dominated by coal at over half of the total energy. Oil is next, at about 30 per cent. Natural gas is far behind, at about 6 per cent—very low by global norms, only a quarter of the global average. 'Modern' renewables are just 3 per cent; and nuclear even less, just over 1 per cent. But this is already changing. Coal will decline, while natural gas and renewables will both gain shares. The current goal is for renewable electricity capacity to triple by 2022 and for gas to reach 15 per cent of the primary energy mix.

> India presents a contrast of a largely agrarian country with a dynamic, relatively modernized and non-industrial, non-agrarian services economy.

As for tomorrow, India will continue to have a striking economic and demographic trajectory that will shape its energy choices as well. Fifty per cent of India will be urbanized in 2050. At the same time, the bulk of the population will be in the largely productive age group of 15–64, and this cohort remains consistent through the decades at about 65–70 per cent, from now until 2050. Meeting the aspirations for a better quality of life for India's young population will require secure, reliable and affordable energy supplies. Starting with $7,000 per capita real GDP (on purchasing power parity [PPP] basis) in 2017, India is expected to reach a per capita real GDP of $10,000 by 2023 and $15,000 by 2032. These are thresholds that typically indicate upper-middle-income and high-income countries. Along with rising incomes—with a young and productive population and a largely urban populace—will come progressive energy choices.

By 2050, India's oil demand is expected to almost double to nearly 9 million barrels per day. Demand for natural gas is expected to more than triple over the same period, and renewables increase to about 6 per cent of the primary energy mix (despite significant increases in absolute percentage terms).

India is not just looking at energy transition, but at an energy transformation on mobility, urbanization and reliability. With 50 per cent of India urbanized by 2050, the choices of a largely young workforce will influence the demand for mobility options and consumer durable goods that affect energy demand. Currently, India's car parc is around 32 per 1,000 people, and IHS Markit expects it to more than quadruple to 132 per 1,000 by 2050. New business models with further innovations to the aggregator model, which provides mobility as a service, will impact consumer choice and energy consumption. At the same time, more electric vehicles and other alternative fuel cars will be on the roads.

With increased urbanization and improved access to electricity, India's per capita electricity consumption is set to rise steeply from 1,145 MWh per 1,000 people in 2017 to 3,895 MWh per 1,000 people in 2050.

> India will continue to have a striking economic and demographic trajectory that will shape its energy choices as well.

All this takes us back to the questions at the beginning of this essay. The first two—India's integration with global markets and development of its own oil and gas resources—are interconnected. Being integrated with the global markets is a great positive. Look at what India's globalized IT sector has done for the overall economy.

In the case of oil, supply and demand are decidedly unbalanced. India currently consumes 4.7 million barrels a day but produces only 865,000. This needs to be seriously readjusted. It is widely recognized that India's high level of oil imports—over 80 per cent of consumption—creates large vulnerabilities in terms of energy security and balance of payments. If that is not addressed, this issue will only become more difficult.

CREATING INDIA'S ENERGY FUTURE

Major steps have been taken in the last half-decade to step up the flows of investment, technology and know-how to ensure that domestic oil and gas resources contribute to India's aspirations for energy security. Continuing to build on those steps and conveying predictability and certainty to investors will create a strong foundation for India's long-term energy future.

During IHS Markit's inaugural India Energy Forum by CERAWeek in October 2017, India's petroleum and natural gas minister, Dharmendra Pradhan, observed that India presents an investment opportunity of $300 billion across the hydrocarbon value chain over the next ten years. Furthermore, the Indian Government estimates substantial investment will be required for meeting India's climate actions.

However, investor perceptions for a country's national energy system tend to persist. This is true for India, as for other countries. For perceptions to change, time and policy certainty are needed.

The changes of the last few years will have to be accelerated in a competitive world in which investors have many alternatives in terms of investment choices around the world, and earn attractive and stable returns for investments that will be operating for decades.

India's energy markets have yet to develop fully such that the right amounts of capital and technology flow into the country. Because India presents one of the most important growth markets for the energy sector and because of policy changes, international companies are again watching India with keen interest. New investments would contribute significantly to India's domestic economy and skills development, to environmental improvement, to retaining talent in the country, and would help manage the costs of imports and protect the balance of payments. Future capital flows will require the assurance of an open, stable and competitive energy system.

Moving in this direction has been a significant achievement for India in the last five years—one noted and respected around the world. I personally have been privileged to observe, up close, this historic evolution unfold and to see the additional respect and appreciation it has brought India from the world community.

There has been a policy push on deepening market-based reform, building infrastructure and enhancing producer access to upstream opportunities and customer access to energy. India has been one of the most active licensors of discovered oilfield and exploration acreage in Asia in the last few years. Now the question is, how soon can India deliver enhanced levels of domestic oil and gas production? Does India have the mix of above-ground enablers and below-ground prospectivity to deliver the next global 'super basin' (an IHS Markit terminology) to be found in India, which shows the promise of a major new increment of production?

Having more players working with different concepts, capabilities and approaches will increase that likelihood.

In terms of the third question—pollution, environment and climate goals—India is also moving ahead on many fronts. One of the biggest environmental scourges in India is the pollution that has accrued from homes across rural India owing to the burning of traditional biomass, which results in serious consequences to health.

> India is not just looking at energy transition, but at an energy transformation on mobility, urbanization and reliability.

The last five years have seen not just a transition, but a transformation, wherein the 'easier' choice in energy supply was replaced by a 'better' choice in energy supply. It also means 'better' in quality of life, which often vast swathes of previously underemployed, agrarian India did not see in generations. In a scheme recognized by the Guinness Book of World Records, India has added as many LPG connections in the last four-plus years, as were added in the sixty years since Independence. Compared to the year 2000, the dependence on polluting biomass and waste in the primary energy mix has fallen from 34 per cent to 22 per cent in 2017, and increased LPG access has played a crucial role in this.

The growth of wind power generation in India was underpinned by the need for electricity for factories whose output was constantly interrupted by blackouts and disruptions in local electricity generation and distribution. Wind has become a significant industry today. In 2017, India added 4.1 GW of wind, ranking it fifth worldwide for additions. Today, India has a vibrant solar sector, encouraged by favourable government policies. Over 9 GW of solar generation was added in 2017, putting India third worldwide in new installations and doubling what had been added in 2016.

But it is important to remember that wind and solar are intermittent power sources, and actual generation is considerably lesser than capacity—differentiating it from fossil or nuclear generation, which runs at far higher levels of capacity. Renewables have to be integrated with other power sources and with a modernized grid to deal with the intermittency.

There is one other critical element for India's energy future—the often-underestimated potential that comes from increasing energy efficiency. India has already embarked on that path. The importance is demonstrated by what has been recently achieved. Between 2005 and 2016, it improved its energy efficiency—as measured in energy per dollar—by 23 per cent.

THE ROAD AHEAD

India is a society that has, throughout history, pioneered markets. One of Asia's oldest roads, the Grand Trunk Road, was a part of the Silk Route. The move to market, such as through market-linked pricing in gas, removal of diesel subsidies and the targeting of subsidies to the poor are all steps that recognize the inexorable shift to markets rather than trying to outguess them. The culmination of these will ensure the growing reliance on markets across all fuels and also the appropriate regulatory mechanisms that enable the move to markets and help ensure that they work well. The time-tested principles that constitute international best practice remain—including diversity of supply, enabling a large number of players, access to infrastructure, standardized measurements of energy and its quality, agreed delivery points and strong regulatory measures that ensure a fair market mechanism which serves the needs of the people and their well-being. Irrespective of fuel type, these principles remain the same.

That India is taking key steps in this direction is recognized worldwide. The pace of completion of the market process is a function of the aspiration to reach a certain energy mix goal that brings together the four energy pillars as elucidated by India's Prime Minister, Narendra Modi—energy security, energy access, energy efficiency and energy sustainability (including meeting climate goals).

The requirements of growth and policy aspirations/targets will accelerate internationalization of India's energy sector and the building of a competitive domestic energy sector to attract the right level of investments. The push for new fuels and new solutions in the Indian energy spectrum through a mix of notifications, pilots and new policies—such as hydrogen fuel cells, coal gasification, bio-Aviation Turbine Fuel (ATF), bio-compressed natural gas (CNG), compressed biogas, methanol, gas hydrates and carbon capture—are significant. This drive has the potential to scale up to a mission mode as a new deal with the New India of the next decade and more. There is a strong case for accelerated collaborations and partnerships that 'future-proof' the Indian energy sector. An adequate balance of soft and hard infrastructure will create the crucible for a fully functional, inclusive, market-based, lower carbon energy system.

The scale of growth resulting from population and economic growth and policy aspirations represent a quantum increase in energy needs. Energy is one equation that India must solve to maintain acceleration on the growth turnpike. This book lays out the elements needed to successfully address the equation for the benefit of the people of the world's largest democracy.

How India goes forward will test the degree and progress of collaboration and partnerships in India—and between India and the rest of the world. And that will be a crucial foundation for India's place in the global community in the decades to come.

2

INDIA'S ENERGY CHALLENGE

Anil Kakodkar

THE GROSS ENERGY SCENE

India represents one-sixth of humanity on a rapid economic development path. Indian youth, globally the largest population that can potentially deliver on large scale transformation, is aspiring to develop the required capability and capacity and in the process, seek a better quality of life for themselves as well as the entire Indian population. Energy availability and access is one of the key factors in enabling this process—as can be seen from Table 1.

Table 1: Per Capita Energy Consumption and
Human Development Index (HDI) Value 2016

Country	Per Capita Energy Consumption (in TOE)	HDI Value	HDI Rank
Germany	3.9	0.926	4
US	7.02	0.92	10
UK	2.87	0.909	16
Japan	3.55	0.903	17

Country	Per Capita Energy Consumption (in TOE)	HDI Value	HDI Rank
France	3.65	0.897	21
Russia	4.67	0.804	49
Brazil	1.45	0.754	79
China	2.22	0.738	90
South Africa	1.91	0.666	119
India	0.54	0.624	131

It is clear from Table 1 that enhancing per capita energy consumption severalfold (maybe four to five times) is one of the minimum necessities for realizing a Human Development Index (HDI) which is comparable to the best in the world.

We use energy in various forms. Electricity is the most convenient carrier of energy with a large variety of convenient end-use devices in almost all domains of energy use—domestic, commercial, industrial and agricultural. The share of electricity use is expected to rise as development progresses. Fluid energy carriers (petrol, diesel, gas, etc.) play a more dominant role in the transportation sector at present, although going forward, we expect increasing use of electric mobility. Similar energy-use transitions continually take place in other segments. For example, gas has become a more convenient fuel for cooking as well as for use in the fertilizer industry, while several low-temperature heating/drying applications use solar energy directly.

Providing energy to users in the required form entails several energy transformation activities, which convert available primary energy forms to more convenient forms and deliver them to users—as can be seen from Figure 1. The basket of primary energy depends on the specific situation of each country. In India, the above data indicates that we derived around 40 per cent of our primary energy needs from coal, 28 per cent from oil, 22 per cent from biomass (including non-commercial primary energy), 6 per cent from gas, 1.4 per cent from hydro, 1.1 per cent from solar and wind and 1.1 per cent from nuclear in the year 2013. Considerable progress has since been made in the use of renewable energy. There is now a major drive to supply clean cooking energy (gas) in place of conventional biomass that has been severely degrading air quality in rural households and affecting the health of people. On the other hand, new technology now holds the promise to enable conversion of biomass of various kinds into clean gaseous fuel for kitchens as well as for replacement of gasoline in its entirety.

A closer look (see Table 2) at the primary energy resources that we can access on the Indian land mass suggests that in the long term, solar and nuclear are the only two sources that can sustainably meet our energy requirements. An important thing to note is that both can be currently used only to produce electricity, and both are non-fossil in nature. Gas hydrate represents a huge potential for the country and could soon become a practical reality. Use of solar and nuclear to produce hydrogen should also become feasible in the near future. Once the related technologies are mastered, India can literally become energy independent.

With declining world energy resources and increasing complexity arising from fast-rising global energy demands, long-term energy security for India lies in developing domestic energy resources and related technologies as fast as possible without getting distracted by global trends that arise from a different demand–supply logic. Luckily for us, the solution to addressing energy-needs sustainability as well as global climate change go hand-in-hand.

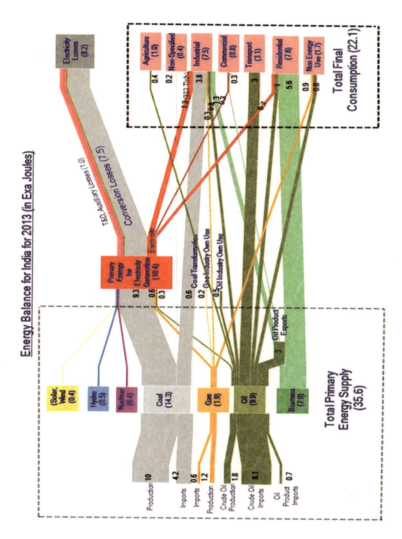

Figure 1: Sankey diagram for energy flow in India

Table 2: India's primary energy resources

Sr. No.	Parameter	Details	Remarks
1	Desirable energy use per year	~ 4 Btoe @ 2400 Kgoe per capita	To reach HDI of 0.9+
2	Fossil energy resources (coal, oil, gas)	Estimated Reserves / Current annual production / consumption Coal ~ 200* / ~0.4* / ~0.45* Oil ~ 0.62* / ~0.05* / ~0.25* Gas ~ 1.1* / ~0.023* / ~0.04* (includes 10% CBM) / *all in Btoe	Most of oil and some gas and coal imported. Import of energy likely to rise steeply. (>5-7 times in 15-20 yrs.)
3	Gas Hydrates	Vast potential (~1700 Btoe). Recent finds in Krishna Godavari Basin offers favourable potential to make a beginning.	Needs special thrust
4	Other Renewable Potential (incl. Hydro, excl. Solar and biomass)	~300,000 MW (peak) 0.2 Btoe/yr	~5 % of requirement
5	Solar Resource	~45,000 sq.km which corresponds to a fourth of barren and uncultivable land in India would be sufficient to meet entire electricity requirements (~20% of total energy requirement)	Needs emphasis on solar thermal (for both electricity and hydrogen)
6	Biomass	~0.1 Btoe/yr * * Better assessment needed. Could be higher.	probably sufficient to meet today's needs
7	Nuclear Resource	Uranium ~ 87 Btoe Thorium >> 600 Btoe	On the basis of nuclear recycle

THREE KEY CHALLENGES

The three key challenges before the energy sector of our country are: Growing energy import bill, addressing short- and long-term energy security and addressing the global as well as local environment and climate change issues. I shall look at these challenges in that order of priority.

At present, a significant part of the energy that we use is imported. Our import dependence has reached 83 per cent in the case of oil, 38 per cent in the case of gas and 25 per cent in the case of coal. Hydrocarbon imports constitute around 23 per cent of India's total imports and could rapidly rise further with growing energy demands. The rising oil import bill and near full dependence on imports is a matter of significant worry in terms of both balance of payments as well as energy security. In this regard potential volatility in hydrocarbon prices considerably augments the associated risk. The Middle East, which continues to be the main provider of oil to India, is becoming much more volatile and the US is becoming increasingly independent of Middle East oil. This could lead to our supplies become more vulnerable. We, thus, have to handle the dual risk of supply disruptions as well as an increasing energy import bill on account of both increasing import quantities as well as potential volatility in prices.

Ensuring energy security is our next big challenge. Reducing dependence on energy imports, raising the level of energy storage, improving assurance of supplies by accessing diverse sources and securing supply lines are some of the key strategies that help enhance energy security. Energy security also needs to be considered in the context of each type of fuel, at least till the time our energy infrastructure becomes flexible enough to easily switch fuel types at the supply end and match the requirements at the demand end.

In the context of enhancing energy security—particularly related to hydrocarbons, which are the main contributors to heavy imports—there are some low-hanging fruits that we can capitalize on in the near term. Apart from a more aggressive domestic exploration and production programme, we should accelerate conversion of other sources like coal and biomass into hydrocarbons. Some potential strategies could be:

1. Coal bed methane.
2. Biofuels (bioethanol, drop-in fuels and biogas) from surplus agri-residue, municipal solid waste, conventional biomass that presently fuels rural kitchens, other forestry residues, surplus grass, etc.
3. Gasification of coal (on surface and in-situ).

> Considerable progress has since been made in the use of renewable energy. There is now a major drive to supply clean cooking energy (gas) in place of using conventional biomass that has been severely degrading air quality in rural households and affecting the health of people.

Promotion of technologies at the user end that offset the use of hydrocarbons, such as solar energy for agricultural pumps, electric mobility, etc. is another important strategy to enhance our energy security and reduce import dependence.

There are significant steps that need to be pursued to realize the results of the above potentialities faster. Redefinition of the mandates of the ministries involved to better streamline policy and decision-making, and bringing in long-term energy security as a driver for shaping the desirable energy mix through subsidy/taxation policies, are some of the important ones. It is important to recognize that left to market forces, the movement in the energy mix may not be consistent with long-term energy security needs.

While coal bed methane does offer a significant contribution to our hydrocarbon energy needs, gasification of coal would offer a much higher potential. Coal gasification is an age-old technology used worldwide, but these technologies invariably use better low ash coals. To address high ash Indian coal, one would need significant India-specific development efforts—a need felt for a long time. It is high time that we mobilize a substantial national R&D and technology development effort to realize this potential at the earliest.

Biofuels offer a much higher potential that can be realized in a relatively short time. For example, bioethanol derived from surplus agri-residue can replace the entire gasoline requirement of the country. Doing so would also significantly contribute to the rural economy, besides addressing the air quality issue. On the deployment side, this is more of a technology management rather than a technology development issue. An integrated view regarding optimization of the scale of the different operations involved in the entire bioenergy value chain—steering rural economy growth in a manner that protects and primarily benefits people at the grassroots alongside having environmental and consequent societal health benefits—would be the key to reaping the benefits of such a possibility.

Contribution of biomass to the national energy basket can be enhanced even further by looking at unaddressed biomass resources, such as the conventional biomass that presently fuels rural kitchens, other forestry residues and surplus grass. Going beyond, the biofuel output can be further enhanced by bringing in external hydrogen to fully utilize the carbon in biomass. Such external hydrogen can be produced by utilizing surplus electricity generation potential that arises these days as a result of increasing integration of variable renewable energy sources into the grid. Steam electrolysis can be looked into for this purpose, for which technology is nearly ready. Going forward, one can expect thermochemical splitting of water to enter the scene, enabling use of solar energy to produce non-fossil hydrogen.

> Solar and nuclear are the only two energy sources available on the Indian landmass that can sustainably meet the desired energy needs of our country.

Continually expanding energy use has a strong link with global warming. While this has been happening in advanced countries, which so far have been the main contributors in filling up most of the available carbon emission space, there is a larger part of global humanity, which is yet to see the full benefit of economic development duly facilitated through augmented energy use. How this can be accommodated within the available space is a major challenge. India being a large segment of the developing world, that is growing rapidly, also has this challenge before it—along with the challenge of reducing the import bill and sustaining energy security. India has already announced its intended nationally determined contributions (INDCs) at the Paris meeting and is aggressively pursuing the necessary actions. Collective INDCs are, however, significantly short of realizing the desirable goal of limiting global warming to within 1.5°C, as per the recent Intergovernmental Panel on Climate Change (IPCC) report. From studies[1] that have been done, it is now clear that nuclear would need to play a significant role along with renewables, in any scenario that would enable us to realize such a goal. This is more so in the case of India, which is a large growing economy. As seen above, use of nuclear along with renewables is also strongly recommended to meet the challenges related to reduction in the import bill and sustained energy security.

SOLAR AND NUCLEAR: KEYS TO OUR ENERGY FUTURE

The data given in Table 2 clearly indicates that solar and nuclear are the only two energy sources available on the Indian land mass that can sustainably meet the desired energy needs of our country, to ensure an HDI comparable with the advanced countries of the world. While the technology to produce electricity using these resources is available, much technology development is needed to derive fluid fuels—which would also be necessary in some segments (transport, for example) of energy use.

While significant progress has been made in the deployment

of solar energy, this has mostly been around photovoltaics, which involve major imports and only a modest domestic value addition. We also need to remain conscious of the additional costs that will need to be incurred as the solar penetration in the current mode improves. Significant additional costs—which could, in fact, be comparable to basic solar investments—could be added to systems and grid costs, to be covered through public money. Looking at the distress it has caused to coal-based power plants, the time has come to decide on policies for power plants that provide baseload power, which play an important role in stable grid operations. There is no sense in putting existing investments in distress—particularly when we are faced with the challenge to grow our energy supply several-fold—as long as they are economically competitive.

Solar thermal has not received as much attention as it deserves. Energy storage, which is a key challenge in steadying solar energy supply, would be much cheaper for thermal storage as compared to electrical storage. Further, at large capacities (greater than a few hundred MWe), solar thermal plants engineered within the country can be more efficient and cheaper as compared to solar photovoltaics. Nearly the entire value addition in the case of solar thermal plants is possible within the country itself, in contrast to photovoltaic units. Going forward, with the development of technologies for advanced thermodynamic cycles (such as the Brayton cycle), one can even realize higher efficiencies at smaller capacities. Further, the solar thermal route would enable use of solar energy for pyrochemical as well as pyrometallurgical processes, in addition to production of electricity. In the context of reducing import dependence of hydrocarbons and finding indigenous energy alternatives, this could be an important long-term option, given the immense solar energy potential in the country. We must recognize that this need is far more urgent for us than for technologically advanced countries.

India has the unique distinction of addressing the challenge of harnessing nuclear energy potential in the most responsible way. Developing this capability has met with several hurdles on the way. Today, we have reached a stage where we are in a position to leverage nuclear energy to address contemporary energy-related challenges that we as a nation, and the world at large, are confronted with. The Government of India has recently approved the construction of ten 700 MWe pressurized heavy water reactor (PHWR)-based indigenous nuclear power plants in fleet mode. Construction of the four remaining 1,000 MWe water-water energetic reactor (VVER) units at Kudankulam, to be built in co-operation with Russia, is also under way. However, much more needs to be done to realize the target of 63 GWe by the year 2032—and it is a crucial target.

Adoption of nuclear energy has been a sensitive issue all along. Looking at the rising energy needs of the emerging economies, it is clear that they will be looking at adoption of nuclear energy, although with some apprehensions. Even countries in the Middle East—the oil providers of the world—are now embracing nuclear energy. With our abundant Thorium resources and related capability, I am of the opinion that we have an opportunity to address the twin concerns of nuclear energy and climate change within the available time frame. This opens up a significant export opportunity for us, leveraging our technological capability built indigenously. We need to get our act together in an effective manner to address this challenge.

Today, coal is the mainstay of our electricity production. While we must accelerate the growth of electricity production based on renewables (solar and wind) and nuclear, we must recognize that coal will continue to be a key energy source for the country, and all efforts towards greater carbon-use efficiency must be well supported.

PETROCHEMICALS

The refinery industry in India has been a success story. We are in a position to compete globally in this segment. While we need to reduce the energy import bill and find ways to increasingly meet our energy needs from sources within the country, we should also aim to become a net exporter in petrochemicals. This would enhance the value addition within the country and at the same time enhance our engagement with the global hydrocarbon sector, even as we seek to reduce energy imports through greater dependence on domestic resources and promote a greater shift to electricity use in the transportation sector. This also has significant importance in the context of national energy security.

MOVE TOWARDS A GAS ECONOMY

The share of gas in India's energy basket (6 per cent) is far below the world average (24 per cent). Going forward, the global outlook on gas seems to be better than that on oil. This may also be true for India. We should also be aggressively pushing exploitation of our gas hydrate potential, which, in principle, could address our growing energy needs sustainably. At this point, shale gas development has made abundant gas available at the source at very low cost and if one were to invest in liquefaction, transportation and regasification infrastructure, one could tap this source economically with low risk of price volatility. Most importantly, gas is much cleaner than coal and oil in the context of CO_2 emissions. Gas is also a much cleaner cooking fuel and needs to be made available in all households in the country, urban and rural alike, to prevent health hazards arising from high particulates in the air wherever solid biomass is being used.

All of this points towards a need for a greater thrust towards a gas economy. This would need a major infrastructure development effort, which should be based on a long-term perspective that looks at potential points of import as well as potential sources and consumption centres of gas within the country, even as we develop individual plans based on near-term economic viability.

JAITAPUR-NANAR SYNERGY

Development of two major energy centres in close proximity, on the west coast in Maharashtra, is in discussion. Jaitapur is expected to house the largest (nearly 10,000 MWe) nuclear power plant in the world and Nanar is expected to be the host for one of the largest (60 million tonnes per year) integrated refinery-cum-petrochemical complex in the world. While such large energy facilities, particularly in close proximity, would naturally be subject to a very detailed scrutiny and due diligence, we need to recognize that the potential long-term synergy between the two would be of great value.

These synergies could be around large-scale production of non-fossil hydrogen, augmented biofuel production and desalination. One could also envision a new model of development, where a large neighbourhood gets supported through corporate social responsibility (CSR) activity.

CARBON CAPTURE AND UTILIZATION

No discussion around energy issues can be complete without talking about carbon capture and utilization (CCU). This is as important as the attempts to reduce CO_2 emissions from energy production. Large-scale economically competitive CO_2 capture and utilization can vacate significant space for the developing world to realize energy benefits for their development. Developing countries should make serious and significant commitments in this regard. Wherever the opportunity exists, enhanced oil recovery (EOR) is a good way for CCU. There are significant possibilities of using CO_2 to create value-added commodities as well as fuels. This effort has already begun in the country and should be incentivized to aid rapid growth. Nature engages in CCU by default. But with greater emission, which nature cannot cope with, we need to supplement natural activities with artificial efforts (that should include enlarging forest cover).

CLOSING REMARKS

The world is at a crossroads today. There is a fear of climate change pushing the planet dangerously close to the tipping point. On the other hand, there is the risk of our being unable to bridge the aspirational gap between the developed and the underdeveloped worlds, which could be a source of potential global conflict. Both are related to the problem of access to energy and the way energy needs are managed.

India representing one-sixth of humanity, with the largest additional energy needs, has to face this challenge squarely—both at the domestic and the international level. A clear national consensus around a well-thought-through overall vision and consequent missions should be the way forward. This needs to be pursued as a national programme and not be constrained by blinkered views in compartmentalized segments of the government and the people.

REFERENCES

1. The Future of Nuclear Energy in a Carbon Constrained World. (2018). [online] Massachusetts Institute of Technology. Available at: http://energy.mit.edu/wp-content/uploads/2018/09/The-Future-of-Nuclear-Energy-in-a-Carbon-Constrained-World.pdf
2. Special Report on Global Warming of 1.5°C. (2018). [online] Intergovernmental Panel on Climate Change. Available at: http://www.ipcc.ch/report/sr15/

3

INDIA TAKES ITS PLACE OF PROMINENCE ON THE ENERGY STAGE

Mohammad Sanusi Barkindo

India is a rising star, quickly becoming the fastest growing energy consumer in the world. The Organization of Petroleum Exporting Countries (OPEC) stands ready to work closely with this fascinating and diverse country in its energy transition, starting with deepening strategic relationship between the two, building on meetings and interactions held so far. Like every country that is undergoing the energy transition, but even more so due to the massive potential impact, there are global implications to India's change.

I want to first thank the Union Minister of Petroleum and Natural Gas and Skill Development and Entrepreneurship of the Government of India, Dharmendra Pradhan, and Prime Minister of India Narendra Modi for hosting several important events in India over 2018—and for their kind invitation to OPEC to attend these events. It has been a stellar year in terms of OPEC–India relations!

This activity also reflects the initiative and visionary leadership of Minister Pradhan, who tirelessly works to ensure India maintains a positive influence on international dialogue in the sphere of energy. I have been honoured to work closely with him and our ongoing engagement will continue in the upcoming months and years.

Like I said earlier, India is a fascinating country, broad and vast, where old and new thrive hand in hand. Maintaining a rich and colourful history, it is at the same time a major global economic player. It is a country of enormous potential, not only because of its burgeoning populace, particularly its large youth population, but also because of its overall rising standard of living.

The OPEC–India dialogue is relatively young having been formalized only a few years ago—in 2015—at the initiative of Minister Pradhan after he attended the OPEC Seminar that year. The first high-level meeting of the OPEC–India Energy Dialogue was held on 15 December of that year in New Delhi. At this initial meeting, the parties agreed to hold a similar high-level meeting every year and to host it alternately in Vienna and New Delhi.

Thus, the second high-level meeting was held in Vienna on 22 May 2017, followed by the third high-level meeting in New Delhi on 17 October 2018. Each year the meeting has improved both in content and interaction.

I want to take a brief look back at that first official high-level dialogue, in which, Minister Pradhan highlighted the importance of OPEC to India, emphasizing that around 85 per cent of its crude and 90 per cent of its gas requirements are fulfilled by OPEC member countries.

OPEC stated that the country is of prime importance as oil demand growth will increasingly shift to India. Minister Pradhan stressed that dialogue will help India and OPEC better understand each other's interests and concerns in order to develop a better working relationship. This inaugural dialogue has turned into a cooperation that is helping ideas turn into concrete actions.

The year 2018 was very auspicious for growing OPEC–India relations. OPEC first came to New Delhi in 2018 to join the sixteenth International Energy Forum (IEF) ministerial on 10–11 April. Minister Pradhan then graced us with his attendance at the OPEC seminar on 20 June in Vienna. Most recently, New Delhi hosted the second annual India Energy Forum by CERA Week held on 16 October, the second technical experts meeting on 16 October, alongside the third high-level meeting of the OPEC–India Energy Dialogue.

The number of meetings over 2017 and 2018 uniting India and OPEC show the rapid pace of growth in the relationship between the two parties. India is an extremely important partner for OPEC—all of us in the Organization are determined to continue strengthening this relationship at both technical and at a high level.

India's growing importance, extending beyond the region and into the world economy, has also led to the country attracting more attention in international fora as well as at dedicated international conferences and symposiums.

Thus, at CERA Week in 2018, much time was devoted to the Indian energy transition with a focus on how interconnected all of our energy futures will be. In addition, it was noted that the oil market has undergone many changes in recent years and continues to face many non-fundamental challenges which are beyond the control of any individual stakeholder, be they geopolitical events, natural catastrophes, technological breakthroughs or climate change—to name a few.

These can strongly affect financial markets and increase the impact on oil. This dynamic has become more apparent recently and makes it more important than ever before to continue to enhance open communication, transparency and diplomacy.

Reciprocity and international dialogue underlie OPEC's work

and these ideals are clearly laid out in its statute. It is also the ideology behind the Declaration of Cooperation process with the Declaration itself having reached a two-year milestone recently.

ECONOMY

India's economy has been experiencing some of the biggest structural changes in a generation marked by bold new reforms. These have placed India firmly on a sustainable dynamic growth path—especially regarding energy.

> India is an extremely important partner for OPEC—all of us in the Organization are determined to continue strengthening this relationship at both a technical and at a high level.

Some of the country's reforms have included demonetization efforts in 2016, the introduction of a goods and services tax (GST) and efforts to diversify the energy mix. These well-structured plans are meant to move the country towards sustainable growth and stability.

The country's young population is becoming increasingly educated and upwardly mobile. This, in turn, will lead to increased demand not just for energy but for goods and services from around the world. In fact, growth in India is expected to be led by domestic consumption and the rise of its middle class.

Up till 2040, strong growth is expected in many sectors, including the transportation sector, as well as an expansion in exports of numerous goods and services. India has a world-renowned IT sector—which today is one of the leading global start-up hubs for technology companies,—and a robust services sector and solid manufacturing base.

The strong increase in foreign direct investment (FDI) shows that the country is appealing to outside investors, which is helping drive growth. Since 2015, India has become a destination point for foreign investors who are now attracted to the country due to the ease of doing business. Prime Minister Modi noted in 2016 that regulatory changes are making India the 'most open economy in the world for FDI', a sentiment echoed by the United Nations, which noted that FDI had jumped by as much as 26 per cent in the first half of 2016.

The country has been able to achieve high GDP growth with low inflation, a well-controlled deficit and a stable exchange rate, which in turn has boosted internal consumption and investment. This is a remarkable achievement for a country of such size and diversity.

With the massive transformation India is undergoing, all energy types will be required to meet its demand.

As an interesting aside, the relationship between OPEC member countries and India goes way beyond just the oil market. Since 2000, trade between the two has grown substantially. India's overall imports from OPEC member countries increased from just over $4 billion to a high of above $170 billion in 2012, before dropping slightly in recent years.

Total imports from OPEC member countries were at $105 billion in 2017, up 25 per cent year-over-year. Meanwhile, OPEC's total imports from India increased from just under $4 billion in 2000 to over $60 billion in 2014. Moreover, OPEC countries' imports from India added up to $44 billion in 2017.

INDIA'S ENERGY PICTURE

India's energy transition is echoing that of other countries but on a larger scale given the size of the country and its burgeoning population. As Minister Pradhan pointed out at the OPEC–India Energy Dialogue in May of 2017, demand will continue to rise for more than a decade.

For this reason, one of the central themes of OPEC's flagship publication, the *World Oil Outlook* (WOO), in its most recent version—launched in Algiers in September 2018 and also rolled out in New Delhi at the second India Energy Forum—is the significant impact of India's economic development on the energy industry.

It is important to examine the country in terms of its future growth on all fronts. India's current population clocks in at nearly 1.4 billion people, constituting nearly 18 per cent of the total world population and making it the second highest populous country globally, only behind China. Of this, 33.2 per cent is urban with the median age young, only 27 years. A 2014 UN report showed India having the world's largest youth population aged between 10 and 24—this generation will be seeking a higher standard of living and greater opportunities and will contribute to a rapidly expanding workforce. These statistics alone indicate a massive future impact on energy and oil consumption.

In a relatively short time—1975 to 2010—India's population doubled to 1.2 billion people. It is projected to be the world's most populated country by the mid-2020s, surpassing China, though its growth contribution will start to shrink. It is expected to be home to more than 1.5 billion people by 2030 and 1.6 billion people by 2040.

This population growth will see accompanying growth in GDP—it will become the fastest growing developing country in terms of GDP—and driving that will be energy. According to OPEC's WOO, we estimate that India's economy will grow at an average annual rate of 6.5 per cent for the period 2017–40. Currently, it has one of the fastest growing GDPs in the world, with real GDP expected to overtake OECD Europe by 2035 and even surpass OECD America by 2040.

Primary energy demand is expected to increase globally by 33 per cent or 91 mboe/d between 2015 and 2040, according to OPEC estimates. India will contribute a massive 24 per cent, or 22 mboe/d, of this increase. This impressive growth reflects the incredible transformation in the Indian economy over the forecast period.

Although coal is still expected to account for nearly half of the energy demand growth in India, the country is the fourth largest oil consumer in the world and significant increases are expected in demand for both oil and natural gas. The country's energy policy also increasingly focuses on nuclear, solar and wind energy.

In this respect, India is one of the countries with the largest production of energy from renewable sources. In fact, renewable energy has been witnessing over 20 per cent growth in the last five years, according to the government's Ministry of New and Renewable Energy. The International Renewable Energy Agency (IRENA) stated in 2017 that hydro (including small hydro) produced 45 GW, followed by wind (33 GW), solar power (18 GW) and solid biomass (9.5 GW).

The country has an estimated renewable energy potential of

about 900 GW from commercially exploitable sources, according to the ministry, and has scaled up its target for renewable energy capacity to 175 GW by the year 2022, which includes 100 GW from solar and 60 GW from wind.

The Government of India stated in its submission to the United Nations Framework Convention on Climate Change on Intended Nationally Determined Contributions (INDCs) that India will achieve 40 per cent cumulative electric power capacity from non-fossil-fuel-based energy resources by 2030.

OIL DEMAND

Crude oil demand growth will increasingly shift to India in the coming years.

According to our WOO 2018, the country's total crude oil demand was 4.5 million barrels per day (mb/d) in 2017, the majority of which was imported. In fact, imports rose from around 1.5 mb/d in 2000 to close to 4.3 mb/d in 2017. OPEC member countries supplied approximately 83 per cent of this. In 2017, India was the third fastest growing nation in terms of oil demand globally, with an increase of close to 140,000 b/d, or 3.3 per cent.

World oil demand is projected to increase by 14.5 per cent, rising from 97.2 mb/d in 2017 to 111.7 mb/d in 2040, according to the WOO. Of this, India alone will account for demand growth of 5.8 mb/d, an incredible 40 per cent of the overall increase.

This represents an increase by over 120 per cent, from 4.5 mb/d in 2017 to 10.4 mb/d in 2040. Thus, its total share of global oil demand will rise from almost 5 per cent to more than 9 per cent in 2040. The country is therefore projected to have the fastest average oil demand growth (3.7 per cent p.a.) in the period 2017–40 as well as the largest additional demand.

Most of India's incremental demand in this time frame will come from the robust expansion of its transport system, in particular road transportation (3.5 mb/d growth in the road transportation sector plus 0.4 mb/d in aviation).

> India is one of the countries with the largest production of energy from renewable sources. In fact, renewable energy has been witnessing over 20 per cent growth in the last five years, according to the government's Ministry of New and Renewable Energy.

India is projected to have the highest total passenger vehicle stock growth from 2017 to 2040 at 8.2 per cent per annum This is due to the relatively low base of existing stock levels and projected high GDP growth. In absolute numbers, this translates to 128 million additional passenger cars in India by 2040.

Additional expansion over the long term is also projected in the residential/agriculture sector (0.7 mb/d), for the industrial use of oil (0.5 mb/d) and for petrochemicals (0.6 mb/d). This brings me back to a crucial point. In order to meet tomorrow's needs in India and worldwide, an estimated $11 trillion in investment is required in the global oil sector up to 2040, which is indeed a massive challenge facing the industry.

NATIONAL ENERGY POLICY

At the sixteenth IEF, Prime Minister Modi stated that India's energy future has four pillars: energy access, energy efficiency, energy sustainability and energy security.

In order to meet this, 'our government believes in an integrated approach for energy planning, and our energy agenda is inclusive,' said Prime Minister Modi. He added that India will be the key driver of global energy demand in the next twenty-five years.

Prime Minister Modi also focused on the over one billion people worldwide who do not have access to electricity and the many who do not have access to clean fuel, making universal access to clean, affordable, sustainable and equitable supply of energy a key part of the country's platform on the road to energy security.

He added that there must be a mutually supportive relationship between producers and consumers. To this end, he commented on the necessity for price stability, stating that 'the world has for too long seen prices on a roller-coaster'.

Minister Pradhan stated at the same event that India is looking for clean, affordable, sustainable energy, to 'transform common lives in India'.

COLLABORATIVE APPROACH

This is where OPEC can be of great assistance. It is our view that market stability is a cornerstone for energy security. To this end, the Declaration of Cooperation, signed by twenty-four OPEC and non-OPEC countries on 10 December 2016, has ably demonstrated the effectiveness of cooperation among producing countries in contributing to market stability.

This collaborative approach has been the lynchpin to

the blossoming relationships between OPEC and non-OPEC participating producers and has promoted exchanges between OPEC and consuming countries.

The historic Declaration of Cooperation is a new entity on the energy landscape. It helped transform the most severe market downturn in the history of the industry—with accompanying layoffs, bankruptcies and economic depression—into a new era of optimism and stability.

Between 2014 and 2016, world oil supply growth went well beyond demand, rising by 5.8 mb/d—demand lagging behind with an increase of 4.3 mb/d. The commercial stock overhang reached a record high of around 403 mb above the five-year average. And the OPEC Reference Basket plunged by an incredible 80 per cent between June 2014 and January 2016.

I want to point out here the serious effect this had on investment, which fell by a massive 25 per cent in both 2015 and 2016, with nearly $1 trillion frozen or stopped. This extremely damaging cycle had the potential to seriously worsen and continue to undermine the future of the global economy, which is strongly linked to the oil industry. The industry itself was on the verge of collapse, which would have been disastrous to both consumers and producers in the short, medium and long term.

OPEC and its non-OPEC partners took this situation very seriously and worked round the clock in the months leading up to the Declaration of Cooperation to try and find a solution. The determination, unending hard work and commitment of these countries to seek a way forward cannot be underestimated. Never before in the history of oil industry has such a collaboration taken place so successfully and on such a large scale.

With the 10 December 2016 decision, the twenty-four countries agreed to take 1.8 mb/d of oil off the market. This was met by immediate relief in the market, which quickly began to come back into balance. The world economy rebounded in kind and world oil demand also rose as a result of the newfound stability in the market.

With the various decisions by OPEC and non-OPEC participating countries over these past two years under the Declaration of Cooperation, we have proven that we can manage both excess and deficiency in the market very quickly and effectively. The mechanism we have established to help stabilize the market has been proven to be both flexible and effective.

The conformity levels of all countries involved and overall success of our efforts has far exceeded the expectations of even the creators of the Declaration, and we remain proud to be a part of these pioneering efforts.

Throughout this process, the input of various consuming countries—India, essential among these—has aided this process, allowing us to incorporate and respond to concerns inside of this strategy.

The Declaration has set the stage not only for future sustainable stability in the oil industry, but has set an example to the world as to how effective such international collaboration can be. To date, we are working on institutionalizing the framework for these efforts, and a draft Charter of Cooperation was endorsed in principle by all countries at the fifth OPEC and non-OPEC ministerial meeting, to be finalized and ratified in 2019.

We remain committed to closely monitoring oil fundamentals and reacting quickly to any changes which may threaten the supply–demand balance, thus serving the interests of consumers, producers, the industry and the global economy at large.

INDIA'S OIL SECTOR

On a mission to India in April 2018, when I visited the first oil well at Digboi in the spectacular state of Assam, I was reminded of just how deep and colourful the historical roots of the industry are in the country. They go back to the early 1880s, with the first commercial well already spudded, incredibly, in 1889, and commercial production taking place one year later.

I was told stories about elephants, which worked in the industry as regular employees for many decades, and refused to work after 2 p.m. when the whistle blew! One of the world's oldest functioning refineries is still in operation at Digboi.

India's oil companies are present in countries around the world with overseas acquisitions playing an important role in the Indian energy security strategy, which seeks to expand the country's global footprint and diversify energy sources.

The country's refinery sector is blossoming, and as of 1 May 2018, it had an oil refining capacity of 247.6 million tonnes per annum, making it the second largest refiner in Asia. It has nineteen public and three private refineries. Indian Oil is going to invest ₹1.8 trillion over the next five to seven years to expand refining capacity. This is supported by the government allowing 100 per cent FDI in upstream and private sector refining projects. These are massive accomplishments which add value and bring jobs to the country.

India was producing 0.64 mb/d of oil in 2018, and has 600 million metric tonnes of proven oil reserves as of 2016, according to the India Brand Equity Foundation. The upstream segment is dominated by the stated-owned Oil and Natural Gas Corporation Limited (ONGC), which owns about 57 per cent of the market. During fiscal year 2017, 540 wells were drilled in the country and in January 2018, after an eight-year gap, the government auctioned fifty-five exploration blocks for oil and gas. ONGC is going to invest $2.73 billion on drilling and gas wells in 2018–19.

Domestic oil companies are focusing on vertical integration for the next stage of growth, expanding into upstream and downstream operations. Efforts are being made to enhance production from brownfields and there is a stronger focus on exploration and development of shale reserves.

There is still great potential for exploration, expansion of pipelines, and expanding the petroleum product distribution network. To this end, many OPEC member countries are investing in India and international oil companies are also very active. We are hoping that OPEC country cooperation with India will continue to grow in the future to the benefit of all our industries.

These efforts show the exhaustive lengths the government and local industry are going to ensure the country develops its own industry in a sustainable way, in its drive to achieve energy security for the people of India.

SUSTAINABLE DEVELOPMENT AND CLIMATE CHANGE

I think it is essential that we, as a world community, always consider the climate change challenge and sustainable development in the context of discussions on energy transition.

OPEC has always been and remains fully engaged with the Paris Agreement. OPEC and our non-OPEC partners in the Declaration of Cooperation will continue to honour our obligation in combating climate change based on equity, common but differentiated responsibilities and respective capabilities.

MOHAMMAD SANUSI BARKINDO »

The country's refinery sector is blossoming, and as of 1 May 2018, it had an oil refining capacity of 247.6 million tonnes per annum, making it the second largest refiner in Asia.

The launch, on 8 October 2018, of an Intergovernmental Panel on Climate Change (IPCC) special report on the impacts of global warming of 1.5 °C above pre-industrial levels and related global greenhouse gas emission pathways brings home the urgency of climate change efforts. However, we should consider that this change must come via several channels, and that those most at risk of the biggest impacts remain disadvantaged populations—particularly in the developing world.

Once again, this massive challenge affecting us all cannot be faced alone. Only a collaborative and collective response is going to guide us in eliminating the 42 billion tonnes of carbon dioxide in annual emissions required to reach the temperature target.

We cannot and will not leave behind those facing energy poverty, which holds back so many from attaining even the bare essentials—such as power and light—and develop a sustainable future for their families. Among these are the approximately 3 billion people without clean cooking fuels and at least 1 billion without access to electricity.

It is estimated that about 244 million people in India live without electricity, the majority of whom are in rural areas, representing a massive challenge. Oil can help meet the goal of eradicating energy poverty within this population as a proven and reliable energy source for example, for mini-grids and fuel cells.

To meet the dual global challenge of climate change and energy poverty, all energy sources will be needed, combined with technologies to minimize and eventually remove the greenhouse gases being released. This should not be about choosing one energy source over another. Each has an essential role to play. The oil industry can play a critical role both in meeting the needs of those facing energy poverty, and combating climate change.

To this end, our industry has always been a technology leader and must continue to be a part of the solution to the climate change challenge. Our civilization's growth and social progress is based largely on the contribution of oil, and this should continue.

The oil industry's cumulative experience and know-how, along with the capacity for technological innovation upon which it is built, can and must be leveraged to help meet these goals.

The industry has made great strides recently in tackling these issues, as can be seen, for example, by the inception of the Oil and Gas Climate Initiative (OGCI) in 2014.

This group of thirteen CEOs of major oil companies is leading a voluntary initiative to 'leverage the industry's collective strength to lower the carbon footprint of the energy, industry and transportation value chains via engagements, policies, investments and deployment.' They are dedicated to the ambition of the Paris Agreement to reach net zero emissions in the second half of this century. This amazing group has already established an investment fund of more than $1 billion to lower the carbon footprint of the energy and industrial sectors.

They are focused on three objectives: reducing the energy value chain footprint, accelerating low-carbon solutions and enabling a circular carbon model. For example, the OGCI companies have, in September 2018, announced a target to reduce collective average methane intensity of aggregated upstream oil and gas operations to below 0.25 per cent by 2025. It supports the development of carbon capture and storage, an incentive that could greatly reduce the carbon footprint of the industry.

The International Energy Agency Greenhouse Gas (IEAGHG), formed in 1991 with fifteen member countries, is funding research into carbon capture and storage and is supported by OPEC, among others.

The World Bank Group started a Zero Routine Flaring by 2030 initiative three years ago, which is meant to remove associated gas produced from reservoirs together with oil. It emphasizes capturing this valuable energy source while at the same time eliminating the CO_2 emissions caused by flaring.

Governments that endorse the initiative agree to provide a legal, regulatory investment-and-operating environment conducive to upstream investments and the development of viable markets to use the captured gas and bring it to the market. There are currently seventy-seven endorsers—including seven OPEC member country government partners—covering about 60 per cent of the total gas flared around the world.

As of July 2018, new satellite data shows a significant decline in gas flaring at oil production sites around the world in 2017. Most OPEC member countries have taken ambitious steps to reduce flaring.

These are some fine examples of the corporate world joining hands with governments, organizations and civil society to find solutions, and the results to date show that elimination of emissions is indeed achievable. We hope very much to see such initiatives increase in size and speed of delivery in the future.

RICH CULTURAL HERITAGE

I want to emphasize in closing that oil will continue to play a critical role in the world's energy mix while India will have a pivotal role in the future of the global oil industry and economic growth.

I also want to once again thank the innovative and forward-thinking leadership of India for its support the OPEC's mission as well as endorsing, expanding and enriching our ongoing dialogue. The famous writer of Indian origin, V.S. Naipaul wrote, 'After all, we make ourselves according to the ideas we have of our possibilities.'

Given the rapid development of this great nation and the vast potential of its young people, India seems to have an endless capacity for possibility, which certainly points to a bright future.

I have always been drawn to India, which is known as a place where colour is 'doubly bright', a country which 'taught us how to count', and which embraces tolerance and gentleness.

May this gem of a country, with its unique history, culture and heritage and its ceaseless innovation, cultural diversity, and boundless ingenuity, inspire us all to continue to work together in the interests of consumers and producers.

LIST OF MEETINGS

2015: First High-level Meeting of the OPEC–India Energy Dialogue, 15 December, New Delhi.
2016: Petrotech Conference, December, New Delhi.
2017: Second High-level Meeting of the OPEC–India Energy Dialogue, 22 May, Vienna.
2017: OPEC–India Bilateral Meeting, New Delhi.

2017: India Energy Forum, 8–10 October (CERA Week), New Delhi.

2018: Plenary Session 1, Sixteenth IEF Ministerial, 11 April, New Delhi.

2018: Indian Minister Dharmendra Pradhan speaks at OPEC Seminar, 20 June, Vienna.

2018: Third High-level Meeting of the OPEC–India Energy Dialogue, 17 October, New Delhi.

2018: Second Annual India Energy Forum by CERA Week, 16 October, New Delhi.

2018: Second Technical Experts Meeting, 16 October, New Delhi.

4

HOUSEHOLD ENERGY TRANSITION IN INDIA AND ELSEWHERE: THE ROLE OF LPG

Kirk R. Smith and Abhishek Jain[1]

Unlike Western countries, India has developed a modern economy, with modern sources of pollution and associated health impacts, even when much of its population has still not transitioned away from traditional household cookfuels—primarily various forms of biomass. When air pollution risks were recognized in the US and Europe in the 1950s, by comparison, household air pollution from cooking with solid fuels was a memory from previous generations. This divergence—with part of the Indian population moving towards modern sources of energy, like natural gas and electricity, while others are stuck using traditional fuels—results in a double health risk from modern forms of air pollution such as coal-fired power plants as well as from household air pollution, primarily in poor rural populations. Currently, estimates are that the total impact is some 1.6 million premature deaths annually—but perhaps more

---

[1] We appreciate comments by Ajay Pillarisetti, Ambuj Sagar and Alok Tripathi.

tellingly, it is thought to be the second most important cause of lost healthy life years in the country, after the malnutrition that causes low birth weight, childhood stunting and anaemia (IHME 2018). A number of other low- and middle-income countries are in similar situations.

Household use of biomass is also understood to cause other social problems. Hundreds of millions of hours are spent by householders every week around the country in gathering fuel and in the extra time needed to cook. It is increasingly recognized that this is a drag on the life of villagers—particularly women—and this time could be used for income generation, childcare, education, and to reduce the burden of rural life. Indeed, in the modern sector, we have become accustomed to technologies being promoted simply as 'labour saving', which is considered a benefit even without direct evidence of how the saved time would be used. Time consumed because of the use of traditional biomass in cooking remains one of largest targets in India (and the world) for labour-saving interventions.

Since the 1950s, there have been efforts in India to promote so-called 'smokeless' chulhas, culminating in the National Programme on Improved Chulha starting in the early 1980s and running till 2003 in its original form with a brief revival around 2009. This approach has been termed as an attempt 'to make the available clean', that is, to burn available biomass more efficiently and cleanly (Smith 2014). In recent decades, however, evidence linking air pollution and health has grown and it is now understood that the necessary emission levels from the cook stoves have to be very low to be truly health protective (WHO 2014). To date, in spite of widespread progress by dozens of researchers, cookstove enterprises, government programmes, international agencies and donors—and hundreds of well-meaning NGOs—no stove system has emerged worldwide that is reliably clean enough while using unprocessed biomass (Jetter 2012). Various processed biomass fuels show promise but have not yet been shown to be scalable with the necessary utility-style support services to enable sustained use of cleaner fuel. Work also proceeds on other fronts, including new developments in photovoltaic-powered cooking systems that show promise.

Meanwhile, India has rapidly developed economically: GDP per capita has grown from $260 in 1980 to over $2000 today (in 2017 US dollars)—a mean annual growth rate of over 6 per cent (World Bank). In spite of the growth of clean fuel in the middle class during this period, however, the rural population was not gaining access to clean fuels, and about 700 million people still had no clean fuel until 2015 (HEI 2018). This has been termed India's 'chulha trap'—that is, a constant large poor population staying behind as the rest of the country makes the energy transition (Smith 2014).

MAKE THE CLEAN AVAILABLE

In the middle of this decade, a new paradigm came to the fore, to break out of the chulha trap. As shown in Figure 1, in addition to continuing to try to find technologies to make biomass clean, greater emphasis is now being placed on trying to 'make the clean available' (Smith 2014). In other words, there is a push to enhance access to well-developed clean cooking systems for economically poor populations.

This approach has advantages over promoting new and novel advanced biomass fuel technologies that need both product as well as customer development. Clean fuels such as liquefied petroleum gas (LPG) are usually aspirational, since poor populations see them in the movies, on TV, and in use by richer neighbours. Given that 60 per cent of the world already uses gas or electricity for cooking, there is little doubt about eventual acceptability for the rest and the ability to cook nearly all cuisines. In addition, gas and grid electricity comes via utilities with major organizations responsible for assuring reliable supply. They may do so poorly in some circumstances but the responsibilities are clear and the entire value chain is already established for improving service reliability.

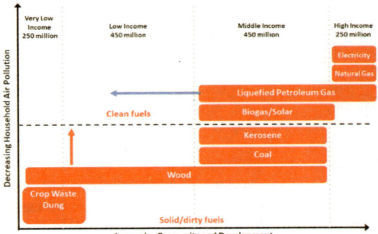

Figure 1: Energy ladder in India. The need is to provide cooking methods for the poor that are clean, that is, fill the upper left quadrant. Two main methods have been attempted— the red arrow, making the available biomass clean; and the blue arrow, making clean LPG available to the poor. Of course, there are policies being undertaken across all the fuels shown.

Source: *Based on figure in Smith and Sagar, 2014.*

The make-the-clean-available approach does not avoid one of the big problems from a health standpoint, which is what the energy field calls 'stacking'—that is, the tendency for households to move only partly to a new technology at first and to continue to use traditional biomass for a period. At least, however, the new technology is clean—that is, it meets the World Health Organization (WHO) indoor air pollution guidelines (Shen 2018). Thus, the more it is used, the more it cleans up indoor air pollution, which is not necessarily the case with many of the smokeless chulhas that have been promoted. In addition, this lag between availability and full use is a common one in health: just providing condoms, latrines, bed nets and institutional delivery services, for example, is not enough. There must be efforts to accelerate the full transition—to enhance usage—and the health sector has much experience in finding ways to do so.

There are three major constraints on usage: lack of knowledge, reliability of supply and affordability. The first two of these are directly amenable to government, private sector and NGO interventions of the types applied in other arenas. The last has been addressed by application of subsidies of various kinds—to encourage poor households to shift to LPG, for example. As shown in the India case below, the current national LPG programme has developed highly creative ways to use what is called 'Digital India', that is, the rapid development of information technology in the population's normal life (mobile phones, electronic bank accounts, social media, etc.) to address the affordability issue. The country is moving towards being able to justify that the taxpayer funds required to promote use of clean cooking fuels among the poor can be considered as a 'social investment' rather than a subsidy, due to its public health benefits (Smith 2018).

KIRK R. SMITH AND ABHISHEK JAIN ▸

THE INDIAN LPG STORY

The Indian Government has supported expansion and consumption of LPG in the country through its public sector oil marketing companies (OMCs) and direct subsidy of LPG, for more than four decades. As a result, more than 50 per cent of Indian households had an LPG connection in 2011 and about 29 per cent of the population was using it as their primary fuel for cooking (MoHA 2011; PPAC 2016). However, since then, the current decade has been by far the most dynamic time for LPG in India.[2]

LPG service improvements have occurred over a number of fronts. To improve availability of LPG in rural areas, in 2009, the Ministry of Petroleum and Natural Gas (MoPNG) introduced a new category of LPG distributorships to make the distributor model economically viable in rural contexts. Later on, in 2016, LPG distributorship guidelines were further streamlined and aimed to improve LPG availability and supply reliability in rural areas by mandating home delivery of LPG.

---

[2] It is useful to explain the special characteristics of India's LPG system, which often do not exist in other countries. First is the concept of 'connection', which means an official sanction for a household to buy subsidized fuel. It is a separate application process in India and, by itself, does not indicate usage. It costs about ₹1,600 ($23) and covers primarily the deposit on the cylinder. Usage comes from purchasing refills as needed, with the cylinders being swapped out—that is, an empty one is exchanged for a full one. The OMCs, therefore, own the cylinders and are responsible for their maintenance. Urban households typically have paid the deposit for two cylinders, which ensures continuity of consumption between refills of cylinders. About 43 per cent of household connections in the country are for two cylinders. Refills are subsidized currently (up to twelve per year) to keep the price at ₹500 ($7.2 for 14.2 kg LPG), irrespective of the international price. The difference in cost is the subsidy paid by the OMCs and the government. All connection and refill transactions are managed by the OMCs who maintain detailed websites and databases, including one of every customer in the country.

In 2012, two major initiatives were introduced regarding LPG. One, for the first time since its introduction, the number of subsidized LPG cylinders available to a household got capped—first to a level of six cylinders annually, then nine, and eventually to twelve—limiting the potential of wasteful consumption and diversion. Two, as part of the project 'Lakshya', the OMCs under the aegis of MoPNG exploited the full potential of information technology by undertaking a 'Know Your Customer' (KYC) drive while simultaneously streamlining and integrating LPG consumer databases among themselves. The OMCs re-engineered their business process to ensure software de-duplication prior to release of the connection with the help of the National Informatics Centre (NIC). The KYC exercise led to identification of about 15 per cent of all connections as potential duplicate or ghost connections. The exercise was also integrated with Aadhaar, a universal identification programme for Indian residents linked to their basic demographic and biometric information and stored in a centralized database (Mittal 2014).

The KYC exercise resulted in streamlined, IT-enabled LPG consumer databases, which became the foundation of another major LPG initiative—first tried in 2013 and later implemented pan-India in 2014–15—the Direct Benefit Transfer for LPG (DBTL), also known as the PAHAL scheme. PAHAL reduced the market price difference between residential and commercial LPG. It reduced the incentive for LPG distributors to divert LPG intended for household cooking to unintended users or purposes by enabling direct transfer of consumption-linked LPG subsidies into the bank account of consumers. PAHAL, covering 140 million consumers during its implementation in less than a year, became the world's largest benefit transfer scheme. The scheme helped control the diversion of subsidized commodities from the distribution value chain (Jain, Agrawal and Ganesan 2018). Unlike conventional reforms for reducing the fossil fuel subsidy, the DBTL focused on improving the efficiency of the subsidy delivery mechanism to decrease the leakage of the subsidized commodity. More importantly, it enables the possibility for the government to selectively target the subsidy to specific groups of beneficiaries, instead of providing it universally (as was the case before it was introduced).

Just as PAHAL implementation was nearing its completion, the Indian Government launched a unique initiative in 2015 called 'Give it Up', a public campaign to urge well-to-do households who could afford their LPG consumption at the market price to give up their subsidy. The campaign was led directly by the Indian Prime Minister; at his behest, well-to-do households could give up their LPG subsidy so that the saved resources could be used to provide LPG to poorer populations. 'Give it Up', a real-world example of nudge theory in action, managed to have more than ten million LPG consumers (about 7 per cent of the consumer base in 2015) voluntarily giving up their subsidy and many more not taking subsidy when first connecting. More importantly, the campaign created an enabling environment for the government to bring in another regulation, later in 2016, to wean away the subsidy from households with an annual income greater than ₹1 million (PIB 2015). However, this is merely the start of what could be done towards subsidy rationalizations and targeting.

In 2016, the Indian Government brought unprecedented focus on LPG penetration in the country by way of the Pradhan Mantri Ujjwala Yojana (PMUY) with an initial budgetary allocation of ₹80 billion (~$1.1 billion). The scheme had an ambitious target to provide fifty million new LPG connections at a subsidized cost to socioeconomically weaker households in three years (PIB

2016). However, the implementation of the scheme was even more ambitious than its target, achieving it in less than two-and-a-half years, which led to a revised target of eighty million connections by 2020 (PIB 2018). On average, more than 50,000 new connections are established every day since the start of the programme making the sheer scale and pace of LPG expansion unprecedented.

Even for the implementation of PMUY, information technology is significantly leveraged for both regular progress monitoring as well as to minimize implementation gaps. PMUY provides connections to the lead female member of the household, linking her Aadhaar number, bank account and the household's mobile number. These data are used to ensure that connections are being provided only to those households which are not existing LPG consumers and which belong to socio-economically weaker sections. As of January 2018, more than sixty million connections have been released under PMUY. Interestingly, efforts to implement PMUY have also led to a significant increase in new rural connections beyond PMUY, increasing the overall penetration of LPG connections to close to 85 per cent of the Indian population.

While PMUY focuses on overcoming the significant adoption barrier of high upfront costs, a high level of LPG use—displacing traditional biomass—is required by the households to realize the health benefits. To understand the impact of PMUY in transitioning households from using traditional biomass, it is important to have large-scale, field-based representative data. One way to assess the situation at the aggregate level is to use the administrative data from the OMCs on various fronts, including the number of beneficiaries across different social groups and refill rates by social groups and regions—and to compare this data with similar information for regular LPG users (non-PMUY). While the government has made significant efforts in enabling greater transparency of LPG-related data through public data portals for each OMC, these outlets are not currently structured to be conducive to obtaining data at the scale or in a form suitable for assessing on-ground realities.

In the absence of such easily accessible and usable data, primary surveys are the main approach to gathering information on LPG consumption, its stacking with traditional fuels, households' cooking energy expenditures and so forth. In 2018, Jain et al published findings based on an energy access survey[3] of ~9,000 rural households in six major energy-access-deprived states—Bihar, Jharkhand, Madhya Pradesh, Odisha, Uttar Pradesh and West Bengal. These states collectively account for about 50 per cent of the Indian rural population. It is the follow-up to the first round of the survey, which was conducted in 2015, that provides the baseline for understanding the impact of PMUY, which started in 2016 (Jain et al. 2015; Aklin et al. 2016). The sampling framework for the surveys was designed to be representative of the rural areas in each of the six states, which have received 60 per cent of the total PMUY connections (PPAC 2018). The following paragraphs are based on the results from this set of surveys.

The two rounds of surveys found that the proportion of rural households of the six surveyed states using LPG had increased from 22 per cent in 2015 to 58 per cent in 2018. Importantly, inequity in access to LPG among different social groups also declined. The proportion of Scheduled Caste and Scheduled Tribe[4] households

---

[3] The ACCESS survey in 2018 was a joint collaboration between the Council on Energy, Environment and Water, the National University of Singapore, and the Initiative for Sustainable Energy Policy.

[4] The Scheduled Castes and Scheduled Tribes are officially designated groups of historically disadvantaged people in India. The terms are recognized in the

who reported using LPG in 2015 and in 2018 increased from 12 to 55 per cent and 8 to 38 per cent respectively, significantly improving LPG penetration among marginalized groups.

Rural populations' aspiration to adopt LPG has also increased over time. In 2018, 83 per cent of households without LPG in these six states expressed interest in acquiring a connection compared to 48 per cent of such households in 2015.

Beyond connections and rising aspirations, the proportion of households reporting LPG as their primary and only cooking fuel also increased from 14 per cent to 37 per cent and from 5 per cent to 19 per cent respectively. Of the total number of LPG-using households in 2018, almost one-third are using it exclusively—that is, no stacking with traditional biomass—up from 22 per cent in 2015.

For non-PMUY LPG users, the survey found a strong correlation between average annual LPG consumption and age of the LPG connections, potentially indicating that full consumption of LPG in new connections takes time to evolve (see Figure 2). Thus, judging the impact of PMUY through refill rates after only two years could be premature. This does not necessarily suggest, however, that the evolution of LPG consumption for PMUY households will be similar to that of non-PMUY households. Non-PMUY households are those that were able to afford the upfront cost of the LPG connection, and hence are presumably better off economically than PMUY households. Thus, it is likely that LPG consumption for PMUY and non-PMUY households may exhibit different rates of change over time.

Constitution of India.

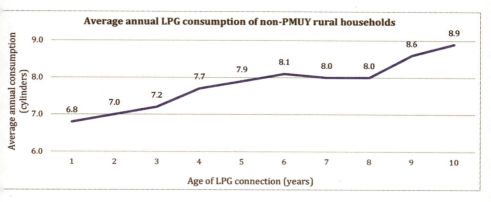

Figure 2: Refill rate versus time since connection for non-PMUY households.

Source: Jain et al 2018

Stacking of traditional biomass with LPG or cleaner options remains a critical challenge from a health perspective. To evaluate if stacking varies between PMUY and non-PMUY households, Jain et al (2018) categorize LPG users into three groups—PMUY households, non-PMUY households with connections up to two years old, and all non-PMUY households—to control for age of the connection. It finds that across states, a higher proportion of PMUY households stack LPG with biomass than their non-PMUY counterparts with similar age of connection. Among non-PMUY households, stacking reduces with the age of connection (see Figure 3).

> The current national LPG programme has developed highly creative ways to use what is called 'Digital India'.

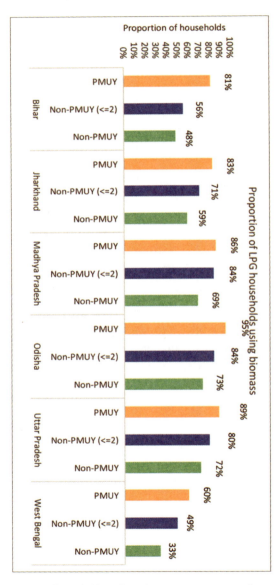

Figure 3: Proportion of households with LPG connections reporting biomass usage:

PMUY; Non-PMUY for less than two years; and total non-PMUY

Source: Jain et al 2018

When asked why they do not use LPG for all their cooking needs, recurring cost and availability of free-of-cost biomass were the most frequently cited reasons by both PMUY and non-PMUY households (Figure 4). The two reasons are somewhat related, of course, for if the opportunity cost of the time spent gathering and preparing biomass is zero or very low, gathering biomass may have no perceived cost compared to purchasing LPG, even with a subsidy. Transitioning to LPG saves time otherwise spent collecting and preparing biomass, preparing traditional stoves, cooking food and cleaning utensils, which blacken when used over traditional stoves with biomass fuels. Providing avenues and opportunities for women to use their newly free time in income-generating activities could help improve the purchasing capacity of the household and give them a means to pay for recurring use of fuel.

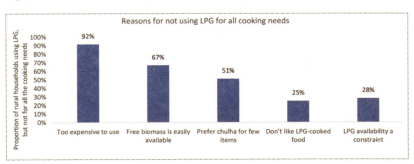

Figure 4: Households not using LPG for all needs mention cost of using LPG and the availability of free-of-cost biomass as the two most common factors preventing their complete transition to LPG.

Source: Jain et al 2018

The PMUY tries to provide some agency to women: LPG connections under PMUY are only given in the name of the female lead of the household and the consumption-linked subsidy is also transferred into the woman's bank account. The survey found, however, almost two-thirds of LPG-using households reported that the decision about when to order a refill is made by a man in the household. This may change, however, as women participate more in household income generation by utilizing time saved due to use of LPG.

Although understanding and attending to intra-household gender dynamics is important, the affordability of LPG remains a significant concern and barrier to its sustained use for all cooking energy needs. Thus, coinciding livelihood interventions, particularly for women, along with PMUY and other LPG initiatives, could potentially go a long way in creating a reinforcing loop. The government should also consider better subsidy targeting strategies to provide differential subsidy support based on health vulnerability, household size and economic situation. At the same time, finding more effective ways of continuing to reduce subsidy for the middle- and upper-income groups would keep the total cost to the exchequer low (Tripathi 2015; Jain, Agrawal and Ganesan 2014).

In all, the progress shown by India on improving LPG access throughout the country, by leveraging—among other things—the window of opportunity provided by lower than normal international oil prices is highly praiseworthy. Provision of connections is the first major step towards universal clean cooking energy for all Indians and early results show that connections are translating into use of LPG, albeit slowly. A challenge ahead is to ensure buffering against a potential ballooning of fiscal outlays towards LPG subsidies with the increase in international oil prices, and the increasing consumption of the fuel.

PROGRESS IN OTHER COUNTRIES

Although India's LPG promotion programme is the largest in operation today, other countries have initiated programmes over the last half-century to promote LPG use among the poor with varying degrees of success. These have covered a wide range of approaches but generally have relied on subsidized access to fuel and distinct from India's current programme, have not included a specific focus on the health benefits of using LPG in comparison to using biomass. Usually, they focus on social development objectives that vaguely incorporate health criteria. Thus, they have been justified on somewhat different grounds. Here we focus on programmes in three other quite different but large middle-income countries.

Brazil: A diverse country, which is heavily forested throughout much of its territory, Brazil has had a long history of promoting LPG use among the poor as part of social development. Beginning in 1973, as part of the arrangement that led to the partial privatization of the national oil company, Petrobras, Brazil began heavy subsidies of the fuel for everyone and worked to standardize LPG supply and prices throughout the country. As a result, by the 2000s, about 95 per cent of Brazilian households reported LPG use for cooking, although fuelwood still supplied about 45 per cent of total cooking energy. This programme was paid, largely, by cross-subsidizing with other petroleum products (Coelho 2018).

In 2001–02, with liberalization of the economy, however, the subsidies ended and LPG came to be sold at market prices. In 2003, a system of vouchers for LPG aimed at the poorest groups was initiated, but was considered largely a failure due to poor implementation and associated corruption. Since 2004, the government shifted to an income transfer scheme for the poor that does not focus on LPG, but on income support in general. Use of LPG has remained high, but there has been little reduction in wood fuel use since 2001 as there had been steadily through the 1990s with the older subsidy scheme (Coelho 2018).

This illustrates a dilemma in development economics between consumption-linked benefits to the poor versus providing general funding to the poor for them to spend as they see fit. The former typically has implementation challenges leading to leakages and inefficiencies. But the latter, in many instances, does not lead to intended outcome of improving use of cleaner cooking fuel. Simply providing money to the poor may be persuasive if LPG purchase related mainly to lifestyle, like clothes or travel. People are much better at prioritizing their needs for these than the government. However, in recent years, LPG is increasingly recognized as being more than a lifestyle issue, as being an important component in health protection and time use—that is, productivity. Everyone must cook and if they are using wood fuel, their health status and productivity are inherently limited.

Clearly, the government has a responsibility to promote the health and productivity of its population, in addition to addressing equity issues surrounding poverty. Increased health and productivity enhance every aspect of economic development. Thus, nudging the population to act in a manner leading to improved health and productivity may warrant linking subsidies to specific products and services promoting health benefits. Promoting use of a clean fuel such as LPG is an example of such a policy objective. Like rural primary health care or primary schools, government expenditures can be justified as social investments and not simply as subsidies for the poor as long as they achieve the intended benefits, particularly at community scale. To do so, however, the subsidy targeting system needs to be quite effective and cannot be granted to everyone—specifically the middle- and upper-income classes, who would use LPG and natural gas anyway. Given the evolution of LPG consumption in Brazil in two eras of direct LPG subsidy and general income support to the poor, it may be prudent for Brazil to consider reserving part of its income transfer scheme again for an LPG consumption-linked support programme by leveraging IT-based targeting of the poor that does not benefit the better off. Such a programme should be framed clearly to be temporary with gradual reduction in support as the poor shift to higher income categories.

Indonesia: Kerosene is another fuel that has been subsidized by many developing country governments for decades as an ostensive social benefit for the poor. Around 2008, the Indonesian government realized that the large and growing subsidy cost for kerosene was becoming a major fiscal burden (Thoday 2018). Being easily diverted to alternative uses, particularly in diesel engines, much of the subsidy was also not meeting the intended objectives. Attempts to decrease the subsidy had led to large public demonstrations, however, as the population had become accustomed to it (Beaton 2017).

In the meantime, however, Indonesia had made great strides in electrification, being well on its way to the current target of ~97 per cent of households having electricity provision at the end of 2019. This was no easy feat, given the archipelagic geography of the country, with over 900 permanently inhabited islands. It meant, however, that one of the main uses of kerosene by the poor—lighting—is increasingly becoming redundant. Everywhere in the world, people are happy to substitute clean and bright electric lights for traditional kerosene lamps and with better batteries and hybrid solar lamps, intermittent power supply becomes less troublesome. Increasingly, the only remaining use of kerosene in Indonesia was thus for cooking (ADB 2016).

In 2007, the Indonesian Government requested the national oil company Pertamina to embark on a massive programme to switch out kerosene for LPG. This programme had a number of innovative aspects, but relied heavily on a steady reduction of kerosene subsidies combined with a slight increase in those for LPG. The net change was designed to be roughly the same for the consumer, but save the government billions of US dollars in subsidy (Thoday 2018). Today, it is thought that some two-thirds of all Indonesian households were connected to LPG over this period, although it is difficult to determine exactly how much change would have occurred without the programme.

The Indonesian programme was initiated solely for budgetary reasons, but over the same period international research had made it clear that kerosene use for lighting and cooking has adverse implications for both health and climate. In 2014, on health grounds, WHO—through its indoor air quality guidelines—recommended elimination of kerosene as a household fuel (WHO 2014). Kerosene's particle emissions are also nearly pure black carbon and it thus has a significant climate forcing impact (Lam 2012).

Although now claiming health and climate benefits, the Indonesian programme was not designed for evaluation of these benefits. Pertamina records, however, indicate that there was a major shift in LPG and kerosene sales, which must be having major benefits for both climate and health.

China: Like India, China had a major programme to introduce improved biomass stoves, which ran from around 1980 to the mid-1990s (Smith 1993). Unlike the Indian programme, however, it is credited as being a major success, introducing some 180 million stoves in rural areas during that period (Sinton 2004) and thus being one of the most cost-effective energy efficiency measures ever undertaken in the country.

As in India at that time, however, pollutant emission reductions were not part of the programme's objectives. Thus, while all the introduced Chinese stoves had chimneys and seemed to reduce indoor concentrations by 40 per cent or so when working well, there was little impact on outdoor pollution. As a result, by 2010, studies were beginning to show that the combination of biomass and coal combustion used for cooking and, in winter, space heating, was responsible for some 30 per cent of ambient air pollution exposures in the country (Liu 2016). One study showed that a major reduction in total exposure had occurred even before the major control measures taken in 2013, due to changes in household fuel that had occurred between 2005 and 2015 because of urbanization and economic growth, not policy (Zhao 2018).

In 2013, due to public and media pressure resulting from winter pollution episodes in Beijing and other cities, China embarked on a major programme of new controls for outdoor air pollution, including a range of actions. In 2017, the newly established Beijing–Tianjian–Hebei (BTH) air pollution control district introduced ambitious targets for eliminating solid fuel use in households across a wide area of that part of the country—covering both biomass and coal, for cooking and space heating (Zhao 2018).

The programme to date has focused on electrification for cooking with induction stoves and heat pumps, and introduction of piped natural gas in villages where possible. LPG is also being promoted, but seemingly less so than the others, although future natural gas supplies are uncertain. Subsidies are provided to households for fuel/electricity costs for a few years, with some uncertainty as to the longer term.

It is ironic from the health standpoint that this large Chinese programme focuses solely on the ambient air pollution impact and does not consider the significant benefits to the households themselves from eliminating polluting fuels, as did the study mentioned above (Zhao 2018).

SUMMARY

From the health standpoint, any gaseous fuel—LPG, natural gas or biogas—or electricity are clean at the household level. Most improved cook stoves still struggle to meet indoor air pollution guidelines, especially with non-standardized biomass being used in reality on the ground. They need improvement in technology, development of value-chains of standardized fuels such as pellets and a strong push on innovative business models to effectively address operations and maintenance and after-sales-service issues. Biogas remains a sound option from a technology standpoint but most developing countries struggle with developing enterprise-led innovative business and operational models to provide biogas as a service. It does not seem to work well to rely on the skills of the households themselves to provide maintenance, repair and supply reliability.

Clean cooking energy could only be provided in a sustainable manner through service-based business models—be it for LPG, biogas, improved cook stoves with standardized fuel, or electricity. LPG and electricity are more promising solutions for clean cooking energy today, because of their service-based business models—

where the energy provider takes care of the supply. These supplies are not the most reliable in rural areas currently but the underlying delivery structure lends itself to scale and improvement.

While a suite of technologies needs to play a role in households' energy transition towards cleaner fuels, following are the key lessons from the LPG programme in India and across the three other major middle-income countries examined here:

- Better targeting of subsidies for economically weaker sections of the population accompanied by even greater reductions of subsidy among middle-class and well-to-do households is important to fiscally sustain LPG programmes.
- Application of modern IT methods offers efficient and transparent ways to administer and target subsidies.
- Given the productivity and health benefits compared to use of traditional solid fuels, programmes can be termed 'social investments', which has a major difference in connotation compared to 'subsidy'.
- Programmes with adequate targeting, such as the PMUY, help reduce the disparity in access to clean fuels across different social and income groups.
- Cleaner household fuels have a strong role to play in cleaning up ambient air pollution in many countries, including India and China.
- In India, Brazil and Indonesia, semi-private oil companies, which are still owned mainly by the government, have the operational scale needed to bring change quickly and respond to national needs for such social programmes.
- Once electrification has developed, shifting subsidies away from kerosene for lighting is good for public health and can lower government expenditures.
- Until households make a transition towards electricity-based

cooking, support for clean fuel for cooking programmes is required to enable sustained use of such fuels to support health and productivity.

In the longer term, most household energy in the world will probably be supplied by electricity, powered by non-carbon sources. In the medium term, however, just as Organization for Economic Cooperation and Development (OECD) countries are adopting to natural gas as an efficient, clean, and lower carbon transition fuel moving away from coal, LPG can serve a similar role for household cooking energy needs in low and middle-income countries, moving households away from traditional biomass.

BIBLIOGRAPHY

ADB, 2016. *Achieving Universal Electricity Access in Indonesia*. Asian Development Bank, Manila, 92 pp.

Beaton C., Lucky Lontoh L., M Wai-Poi, 2017. 'Indonesia: Pricing Reforms, Social Assistance, and the Importance of Perceptions', in *The Political Economy of Energy Subsidy Reform*, G. Inchauste and D.G. Victor, eds, World Bank, Washington, DC, pp. 133–208.

Coehlo, 2018. 'The Energy Transition History of Fuelwood Replacement for Liquefied Petroleum Gas in Brazilian households from 1920 to 2016', *Energy Policy* 123: 41–52.

HEI, 2018. *State of Global Air 2018*. Health Effects Institute, Boston, available from: www.stateofglobalair.org.

IHME, 2018, Global Burden of Disease website, accessed on 1 November 2018, https://vizhub.healthdata.org/gbd-compare/

Jain A., S Agrawal, K Ganesan, 2014. *Rationalising Subsidies, Reaching the Underserved*. Council on Energy, Environment and Water, New Delhi.

Jain A., S Agrawal, K Ganesan, 2018. 'Lessons from the World's Largest Subsidy Benefit Transfer Scheme', in J. Skovgaard, and H. Asselt (eds), *The Politics of Fossil Fuel Subsidies and their Reform*. Cambridge: Cambridge University Press, pp. 212–228. doi:

10.1017/9781108241946.014.

Jain A., S Ray, K Ganesan, M Aklin, C Cheng, J Urpelainen, 2015. *Access to Clean Cooking Energy and Electricity: Survey of States*. Council on Energy, Environment, and Water, New Delhi

Jain A., S Tripathi, S Mani, S Patnaik, T Shahidi, K Ganesan, 2018. *Access to Clean Cooking Energy and Electricity: Survey of States 2018*. Council on Energy, Environment, and Water, New Delhi

Jetter J, Y Zhao, K.R. Smith, B Khan, T Yelverton, P DeCarlo, M Hays, 2012, 'Pollutant emissions and energy efficiency under controlled conditions for household biomass cookstoves and implications for metrics useful in setting international test standards', *Environ Sci Tech*. 46,10827–10834.

Lam N.L., Y Chen, C Weyant, V Venkataraman, P Sadavarte, M.A. Johnson, K.R. Smith, B.T. Brem, J Arineitwe, J.E. Ellis, T.C. Bond, 2012, 'Household light makes global heat: High black carbon emissions from kerosene wick lamps', *Environ Sci Technol* 46 (24): 13531–13538.

Liu J, D.L. Mauzerall, Q Chen, Q Zhang, Y Song, W Peng, Z Klimont, X Qiu, S Zhang, M Hu, K.R. Smith, T Zhu, 2016, 'Air pollutant emissions from Chinese households: A major and under-appreciated ambient pollution source', *Proc Nat Acad of Sci*, 113(28):7756-61.

Mittal N, 2014 Case Studies on e-Governance in India-Project Lakshya, National Institute of Smart Governance, New Delhi.

PIB, 2015, Benefit of LPG subsidy will not be available if the consumer or his/her spouse had taxable income of more than Rs Ten lakh in previous financial year. Available at: http://pib.nic.in/newsite/PrintRelease.aspx?relid=133955 (accessed on 22 November 2018).

PIB, 2016, Pradhan Mantri Ujjwala Yojana: A Giant Step Towards Better Life For All. Available at: http://pib.nic.in/newsite/printrelease.aspx?relid=148971 (accessed on 22 November 2018).

PIB, 2018, Cabinet approves enhancement of target under Pradhan Mantri Ujjwala Yojana. Available at: http://pib.nic.in/newsite/PrintRelease.aspx?relid=176351 (accessed on 22 November 2018).

PPAC, 2016, LPG Profile (Data on LPG Marketing) as on 01.04.2016, Petroleum Planning and Analysis Cell, available at http://www.ppac.

gov.in/WriteReadData/userfiles/file/DataonLPGMarketing.pdf (accessed on 22 November 2018).

PPAC, 2018, LPG Profile (Data on LPG Marketing) as on 01.07.2018, Petroleum Planning and Analysis Cell. Available at http://ppac.org.in/WriteReadData/Reports/201809060351030270231LPG1July2018.pdf (accessed on 22 November 2018).

Shen G, Hays, MD, K.R. Smith, C Williams, J.W. Faircloth, J.D. Jetter, 2018, 'Evaluating the performance of household liquefied petroleum gas cookstoves', *Envir Sci and Tech* 52: 904-915.

Sinton J.E., K.R. Smith, J.W. Peabody, Y Liu, X Zhang, R Edwards, Q Gan, 2004, 'An Assessment of Programs to Promote Improved Household Stoves in China', *Energy for Sustain Devel* 8(3):33-52.

Smith, K.R., S.H. Gu, K Huang, D.X. Qiu, 1993, '100 Million Improved Stoves in China: How Was It Done?' *World Development* 21(6): 941-961

Smith K.R., A Sagar, 'Making the clean available: Escaping India's chulha trap', *Energy Policy* 75: 410–414, 2014.

Smith K.R., 2018, Pradhan Mantri Ujjwala Yojana: Transformation of Subsidy to Social Investment in India, Ch 29 in Debroy B, Gangul A, Desai K (eds) *Making of New India: Transformation Under Modi Government*, Dr. Syama Prasad Mookerjee Research Foundation and Wisdom Tree, New Delhi; 401-410.

Thoday K, P Benjamin, M Gan, E Puzzolo. 2018, 'The Mega Conversion Program from kerosene to LPG in Indonesia: Lessons learned and recommendations for future clean cooking energy expansion', *Energy for Sustainable Development*, in press.

Tripathi A, A.D. Sagar, K.R. Smith, 2015, 'Promoting clean and affordable cooking: Smarter subsidies for LPG', *Economic & Political Weekly*, 50(48): 81-84.

WHO, 2014, *Indoor Air Quality Guidelines: Household Fuel Combustion*; World Health Organization: Geneva, Switzerland.

Zhao B, H Zheng, S Wang, K.R. Smith, X Lu, K Aunan, Y Gu, Y Wang, D Ding, J Xing, X Fu, X Yang, K.N. Liou, J Hao, 2018, 'Change in household fuels dominates the decrease in PM2.5 exposure and premature mortality in China in 2005-2015', *Proc. Natl. Acad. Sci.* www.pnas.org/cgi/doi/10.1073/pnas.1812955115

5

JOURNEY TOWARDS A GAS-BASED ECONOMY: DECARBONIZING INDIA FOR A SUSTAINABLE FUTURE

Dharmendra Pradhan

INTRODUCTION

Choosing the appropriate primary energy mix for fuelling the economy of a country is among the most critical decisions that governments and policymakers across the world have to make in the twenty-first century. People, in general, and the youth, in particular, have become vocal about their aspirations. At the same time, environmental concerns can no longer be cast away as inconsequential in the perennial growth versus sustainability debate. If anything, the growing frequency of natural disasters attributable to anthropogenic factors, such as the devastating floods in the southern Indian state of Kerala in August 2018, make it imperative that governments take the lead in mitigating and managing the adverse fallouts of climate change—while also delivering sustainable growth to the citizenry.

THE PRIME MINISTER'S VISION OF A GAS-BASED ECONOMY

When a new government assumed office in May 2014 under the leadership of Prime Minister Narendra Modi, it confronted the classic fuel conundrum—the most eco-friendly energy sources are not the easiest or the most economical to extract, exploit and deploy on the scale that a large, populous country like India needs. Domestic oil and gas production had plateaued. To make matters worse, global crude prices were reaching record-high levels. Faced with the daunting challenge of leading India's highly import-dependent petroleum sector, I sought, early on, the counsel of the Prime Minister on the way forward. The Prime Minister was characteristically forthright, foresighted and pragmatic in his guidance and gave several pointers to work on. One of them was to usher in a gas-based economy in the country. Prime Minister Modi suggested that India must work towards three broad and interrelated outcomes—one, increase the share of natural gas in India's primary energy mix from about 6 per cent in 2015 to 15 per cent by 2030; two, develop critical infrastructure to boost usage of gas in the economy; and, three, develop policy, regulatory and fiscal frameworks such that natural gas acts as an enabler for India to meet its targets under the CoP-21 Paris Agreement.

STEPS TAKEN ON THE SUPPLY SIDE

We began in right earnest. It started with taking a long and hard look at the prevailing gas industry scenario. We held extensive discussions with stakeholders and identified key areas on both the supply side and the demand side, which merited plugging gaps and reworking the policy framework. This also meant that we had to prioritize and take due care to ensure that the dynamics and the equilibrium of the prevailing gas industry did not get disrupted, thus negatively impacting the country's economy.

Historically, the pricing of domestically produced natural gas has been a multifaceted issue in India, mainly due to the fact that most of it is consumed in subsidized end-use sectors of fertilizers, power generation and in city gas distribution (CGD). We revisited the gas pricing guidelines and came out with new domestic natural gas pricing guidelines for 2014, which were implemented prospectively with effect from November 2014. Under these guidelines, the domestic gas price is calculated biannually as the weighted average price of four global benchmarks—the US-based Henry Hub, the Canada-based Alberta Gas, the UK-based National Balancing Point (NBP) and Russian Gas—applicable to all sectors uniformly. This new formula has been well received and is generally regarded as a win-win proposition for gas consumers and producers alike.

Natural gas demand in our country runs far ahead of supply more than half of India's total gas consumption of about 145 million metric standard cubic metres per day (mmscmd) in 2017-18 had to be met through–liquefied natural gas (LNG) imports. This is due to limited domestic gas production. It is important for gas producers to realize remunerative, market-linked pricing to encourage domestic gas production. The government brought in a slew of policy measures to make investment in domestic gas production viable and attractive.

In March 2016, we granted marketing rights—including pricing freedom—to operators for the gas produced from high pressure, high temperature, deepwater and ultra-deepwater areas. A ceiling price—arrived at on the basis of landed price of alternative fuels—for gas produced in this manner was also kept in order to balance the requirements of consuming sectors. Some more significant reforms have been introduced in the upstream exploration and production sectors to incentivize gas production from onshore and offshore fields. In March 2016, we also notified the Hydrocarbon Exploration and Licensing Policy (HELP), which is based on a revenue sharing model wherein explorers offering a higher share of oil and gas to the government are awarded blocks. The salient features of HELP include a single licence for exploration and production of conventional and unconventional hydrocarbons, like for shale oil and gas. Also included as part of HELP is an open acreage licensing policy (OALP) wherein investors can carve out their areas of interest for exploration and production of oil and gas and submit an expression of interest at any time during the year. HELP has an easy-to-administer revenue sharing model and a guarantee for operators to have marketing and pricing freedom for crude oil and natural gas.

We launched the Discovered Small Fields (DSF) Policy in May 2016 with the motive of extracting hydrocarbons from the unmonetized small oil/gas discoveries available in the country. It provides an easy investment option for new and existing players with minimal risk. Round one of the DSF bid was a runaway success, wherein thirty contracts were awarded to twenty companies—out of which thirteen were new entrants in the exploration and production sector. The first oil/gas from a DSF is expected as early as 2019–20. We have now rolled out DSF bid round II in which about sixty discoveries are on offer.

India is a coal-rich country with the world's third largest coal reserves. Yet, for various reasons, we have not been able to develop a robust coal bed methane (CBM) sector till now—which could have given a boost to domestic natural gas output. In order to change things around the CBM sector, we brought a policy framework for early monetization of CBM in April 2017, which provides marketing and pricing freedom for CBM and streamlines operational issues.

We have also managed to put coal to uses that were hitherto unheard of in India. The eastern Indian state of Odisha has sizeable reserves of coal—much of it low quality with high ash content. We gasified this coal to produce syngas, which could act as feedstock for fertilizer plants. In November 2015, a joint venture of four state-run firms started work on setting up India's first-ever coal gasification-based fertilizer unit with a nameplate capacity of 1.27 million metric tonnes per annum (mmtpa) of urea. This ambitious project, upon its completion in 2022, will produce 2.38 mmscmd syngas and enable saving LNG imports worth an estimated ₹1,230 crore annually.

Yet another initiative to boost the supply side for natural gas is compressed biogas (CBG). I have always believed that apart from energy, agriculture is the other key area pivotal to sustaining India's growth rate. We need a healthy agriculture sector to build a strong and prosperous India. While India is self-reliant for its food requirements, we have to depend on imports to meet more than 80 per cent of our crude oil needs. CBG is a much cheaper and cleaner alternative to petrol or diesel and has huge potential to becoming the fuel of the future. In October 2018, our state-run oil marketing companies (OMCs) launched an initiative named Sustainable Alternative Towards Affordable Transportation (SATAT) for promoting CBG in the transport sector. Under this scheme, OMCs offer offtake and remunerative prices for procurement of CBG to attract small entrepreneurs to invest in CBG plants. OMCs, in turn, will market CBG through their retail outlet network across the country to end consumers. CBG can be produced from raw materials such as agricultural waste, animal dung, municipal solid waste, sewage, green waste, food waste and press mud. As per available estimates, there is a total potential of 62 mmtpa CBG in the country from various feedstock. We have targeted to set up 5,000 CBG plants by March 2023 at an investment of around ₹175,000 crore.

The efforts undertaken over the past four and a half years—to bolster the country's gas and LNG infrastructure—are the most critical from a long-term perspective. In May 2014, India had about 15,000 km of cross-country gas pipeline network developed over the previous three to four decades. This would easily pale in comparison to some large gas-consuming countries—say, for example, the US (2 million km), Russia (160,000 km), China (74,000 km), the UK (28,000 km) and Germany (27,000 km). Even similarly placed developing economies like Argentina (30,000 km), Mexico (18,000 km) and Brazil (17,000 km) had a much larger gas network. Worse still, our gas pipeline network was rather skewed with most pipelines concentrated in a few states in western, northern and central India. Other regions, notably eastern India, had practically no presence on India's gas map.

Historically, gas supply would follow demand in India—which meant that gas pipelines were laid well after the anchor consuming industries were identified and contractual arrangements done. We recognized that accessibility is the single most important enabler that spurs gas demand, and took steps accordingly. One, the government gave a renewed thrust to completing the National Gas Grid (NGG) by doubling the gas pipeline network to 30,000 km in a time-bound manner. The Petroleum and Natural Gas Regulatory Board (PNGRB), India's statutory regulator for the midstream and downstream sectors, was tasked with reviewing the progress on unfinished segments of the NGG and optimizing the same based on fresh demand estimations. The ministry engaged provincial governments proactively to secure their support for pipeline construction in the country. Second, and more importantly, we turned conventional wisdom on its head by pursuing gas supply ahead of its demand. The rationale was simple—if gas is accessible in a new area, demand would follow. It is with this reasoning that the government decided to invest, for the first time ever, in the construction of an ambitious new gas pipeline that would put five eastern states on the NGG. We are extending 40 per cent viability gap funding (VGF) amounting to ₹5,176 crore to the Jagdishpur–Haldia and Bokaro–Dhamra pipeline (JHBDPL), more popularly known as the Pradhan Mantri Urja Ganga—the construction of which is progressing rapidly.

JHBDPL/Barauni–Guwahati Pipeline Network

Figure 1

Source: *Gas Authority of India Limited*

Earlier, in August 2018, we set up Indradhanush Gas Grid Limited (IGGL)—a new joint venture of five state-run firms to construct a 1,656 km gas pipeline, which will connect all eight states in India's Northeast with the NGG. Here, too, we chose to go ahead with the project in the interest of promoting gas usage free of internal rate of return (IRR) considerations.

LNG trade has increased significantly over the years with imports rising year-over-year. With the LNG market gradually becoming more liquid, spot and short-term trade now constitutes more than a quarter of all LNG volumes traded. This trend is likely to further accelerate in the future. We have placed a lot of emphasis on greenfield and brownfield expansion of LNG regas capacity in the country. Work on several new LNG import terminals, located on both the west and east coasts, is under way and we expect our regas capacity to double from 26 mmtpa presently to 55 mmtpa by 2022. Two new onland LNG import terminals in Mundra (Gujarat) and Ennore (Tamil Nadu) are expected to become operational within the current fiscal year.

Of late, India has also successfully diversified its LNG sourcing. It was a matter of great pleasure for me to receive the first ever long-term LNG cargoes from the US and Russia at Indian import terminals in 2018. These new beginnings strongly consolidate India's energy security needs.

> March 2016, we also notified the Hydrocarbon Exploration and Licensing Policy (HELP).

INDRADHANUSH GAS GRID LIMITED (IGGL)
Connecting India's Northeast to the National Gas Grid

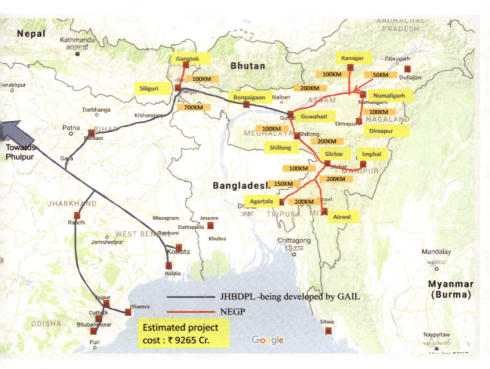

Pipeline length 1656 km

Estimated cost ₹9,265 crore.

- Central oil and gas PSUs, viz. ONGC, OIL, GAIL, IOCL and NRL have signed an MoU to establish IGGL for developing a gas grid system within the North East Region.
- NER grid will connect all the states of North East—Assam, Sikkim, Mizoram, Manipur, Arunachal Pradesh, Tripura, Nagaland and Meghalaya.
- Cities covered—Itanagar, Dimapur, Imphal, Aizwal, Agartala, Silchar, Shillong and Gangtok

Figure 2

Source: *Gas Authority of India Limited*

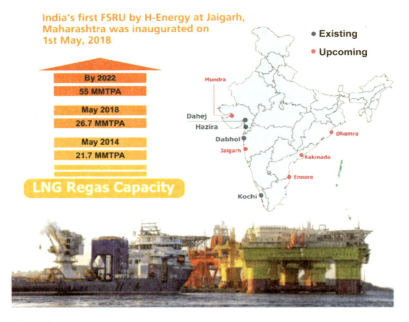

Figure 3

Source: *Ministry of Petroleum and Natural Gas*

STEPS TAKEN ON THE DEMAND SIDE

There have been some equally path-breaking measures on the demand side for natural gas as well. Among these, progress achieved in the CGD sector has truly been a satisfying success story. City distribution networks have the potential to dramatically increase gas consumption in India. CGD entities supply natural gas to household kitchens in the form of piped natural gas (PNG) and to vehicles in the form of compressed natural gas (CNG). Plus, when gas is supplied to small- and medium-sized industrial units as well as commercial units located in urban centres, it often replaces more polluting fuels like coal, furnace oil, naphtha, diesel and the like. Despite the obvious advantages of gas as an environment-friendly fuel, somehow the CGD sector had never received the mindshare that it deserves.

We decided to change India's CGD narrative by restoring focus on natural gas as a fuel that enhances the quality of life of the common man. What brought about this change? Let me share an anecdote. Sometime in mid-2014, when I had just taken up this ministerial assignment, I happened to meet an auto-rickshaw driver. When he learnt that I was the new petroleum minister, he pleaded with me not to increase the price of gas. For him, CNG price in Delhi determined his daily livelihood and the economic well-being of his family. More often than not, auto-rickshaw drivers and taxi drivers lead a hard life in India and are, therefore, anxious for every additional penny earned or saved. When I enquired about the economics of CNG vis-à-vis diesel, they save at least ₹200 every day—or about ₹5,000 every month—simply by using CNG. I understood the centrality of CNG in that auto-rickshaw driver's life and that lesson has stayed with me since. The effect of cost-effective, clean fuel on a common man's life triggered my interest to embark on a transformative journey with the CGD sector.

Over the past four and a half years, the government has taken a series of steps to launch the CGD sector into a high growth trajectory. We began by placing gas supplies for the PNG (domestic) and CNG (transport) segments of the CGD sector in the 'no cut' category, and giving it the highest priority while allocating domestic gas. This ensured that the comparatively lower-priced domestic natural gas is always available for meeting PNG and CNG requirements across the country. On some occasions, this called for diverting domestic gas supply from other sectors causing heartburn to the affected consumers—nevertheless, we didn't shy away from doing that. We enlisted the support of other central ministries to push the cause of CGD. In March 2017, the defence ministry issued guidelines for use of PNG in the residential areas and unit lines of defence establishments. In June 2017, CGD was granted public utility status. In August 2017, government-run companies were instructed to have provisions for PNG in their residential complexes. Further, we worked with the PNGRB to make our CGD sector more investor friendly. Extensive consultations were held with stakeholders, including state governments, before finalizing the districts to be offered for development of gas distribution networks. The bidding parameters were rationalized to encourage wider participation of potential investors/bidders for enhancing competition. The results have been phenomenal with PNG and CNG numbers expanding at a rapid pace. Between April 2014 till the end of September 2018, the number of CNG stations in the country has gone up by 79 per cent standing at 1,450 stations. Also, the number of domestic PNG connections have grown from 24.72 lakh to 47.09 lakh over the same period which marks a 90 per cent growth.

> We decided to change India's CGD narrative by restoring focus on natural gas as a fuel that enhances the quality of life of the common man.

CGD STATISTICS IN INDIA
(As on 01.12.2018)

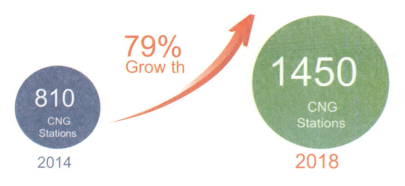

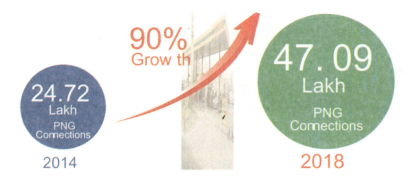

Figure 4

Source: *Petroleum and Natural Gas Regulatory Board (PNGRB)*

BRINGING HALF THE COUNTRY ON THE CGD MAP

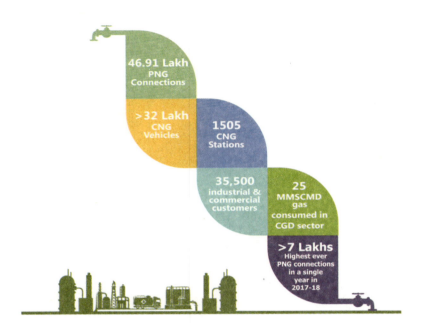

Figure 5

Source: *Petroleum Planning & Analysis Cell*

In 2018–19, Indraprastha Gas Limited (IGL) added over one lakh new PNG connections within the Delhi-NCR region in a record time of seven months. The ninth CGD bidding round concluded in October 2018 was India's largest ever with as many as 174 districts being awarded for CGD development—this would attract an investment of approximately ₹70,000 crore. The tenth CGD bidding round covering 124 districts is presently under way and is expected to attract an investment of another ₹50,000 crore.

After the conclusion of this round, India will cumulatively have CGD infrastructure spread over 402 districts with the potential to cover half the country and reaching more than 70 per cent of the population.

POWERING INDIA

Covered Under CGD	District	GAs	Population	Percentage Area Coverage of India
Till May 2014	66	34	9.0%	2.71%
May 2014 to July 2018	70	58	10.8%	8.29%
9th Bidding Round	174	86	26.4%	23.82%
10th Bidding Round	124	50	24.2%	17.92%
Total (After 10th Bidding Round)	402*	228	70.5%	52.74%

CGD: City Gas Distribution ; GAs: Geographical Areas   *Completed

Figure 6

Source: *Petroleum and Natural Gas Regulatory Board (PNGRB)*

Together with the existing CNG stations and the ones expected under the ninth and tenth rounds, India is looking at a robust infrastructure of about 10,000 CNG stations in ten years from now. Expectedly, these developments in India's CGD space have received a positive response from the industry. The government has given a firm message that CNG is not merely a transition fuel. The response from leading auto-manufacturers has been encouraging and they are coming out with factory-fitted CNG vehicles.

Looking at the growing use of LNG in the transportation sector worldwide, especially in the US and China, we are promoting LNG as a transport fuel for long-haul trucking along expressways, industrial corridors and inside mining areas. Limited trials involving public transport buses running on LNG have also taken place. At least two Indian LNG import terminals already have functional truck loading capabilities, which can support LNG distribution for retail applications, including transport, power and industrial uses. Then there is the upcoming industry of small-scale LNG, which has a scalable, 'plug-and-play' model—this could potentially transform electricity access in remote places by facilitating off-grid power generation. Going forward, we would like to adopt such approaches to boost gas consumption in the country while also lending a helping hand to the environment.

Some other interventions of the government to address demand-side issues in our gas industry are either under implementation or have begun to show results. Beginning July 2015, the government started a scheme whereby domestic gas pooled with imported LNG is supplied to fertilizer units across the country. This has increased domestic urea production by about 2 million tonnes annually. While this has led to substantial savings for the government on account of lower urea import, we have also been able to utilize an additional 3–4 mmscmd gas through this arrangement. Then, over the past few years, Indian companies have successfully renegotiated LNG contracts with overseas suppliers, facilitated by G2G (government to government) intervention wherever needed, so that the imported gas remains affordable and price-competitive for Indian consumers. The renegotiation for long-term LNG from Qatar in December 2015, in particular, saved significant take-or-pay penalty for Indian gas consumers. India has linked its domestic gas prices with the global gas market and is moving towards creating a transparent, fair and real-time mechanism for gas price discovery. The government is working on setting up the country's first-ever gas trading exchange. An efficient gas trading hub would not just attract more buyers and sellers in the marketplace and thus help expand the overall gas pie but also elevate the credibility of the Indian gas industry globally. While the task is onerous, looking at the limited number of market participants active at present—as also the limited infrastructure connected on NGG—we are determined to make a start howsoever modest it may seem.

WHY WAS GAS ECONOMY SUCCESSFUL IN GUJARAT BUT UNABLE TO TAKE OFF IN THE REST OF INDIA?

It may be useful at this juncture to recall that in 2013 the share of natural gas in India's primary energy mix was slightly more than 10 per cent, largely on the back of one prolific gas field in the eastern offshore basins. This came down to about 6 per cent by 2015. At the same time, the share of natural gas in the primary energy mix of the western state of Gujarat has been 26 per cent for several years now. So, what are the learnings from Gujarat's success on the gas front that could be replicated for the rest of the country? In my assessment, the foremost was addressing supply- and demand-side issues in tandem to foster a gas-based economy. With the hand-holding of the state government, the state-owned Gujarat State Petroleum Corporation (GSPC) created 2,600 km of gas pipeline grid within the state. The state also made full use of its coastal location and encouraged setting up of LNG infrastructure to increase gas consumption. Today, the country's two largest LNG regasification terminals (Dahej and Hazira) are functioning in the state with a third (Mundra) on the verge of starting commercial operations. Additionally, another two regasification terminals (Jaffrabad and Chhara) are at various stages of planning or construction. Long before CGD became a buzzword, Gujarat took the lead in CGD business in the 1970s and 1980s—today it has the largest share of CNG stations (32 per cent) and PNG connections (42 per cent) in the country. Gujarat was also a pioneer in gas based power generation—19 per cent of installed power capacity in the state is gas-based compared to 8 per cent nationally. Gujarat has been a power-surplus state for many years now and has consistently ranked among the top business-friendly states in the country, which has helped attract investments. The overall package that the state offers makes for a compelling business proposition for large industrial units to set up base in the state, which then act as anchor consumers for the gas industry. Although not every state has the first-mover advantage, the strategic location or the financial wherewithal that Gujarat possesses, however, some of these initiatives can surely be emulated in other parts of the country.

BENEFITS OF A GAS-BASED ECONOMY AND THE WAY FORWARD

Most of the measures that were discussed in the above paragraphs have been welcomed by the gas industry stakeholders at large. The overall consumption of natural gas in our economy has shown an increasing trend over the past four years but this is mostly on account of increasing imports. While I believe India is on the right track to transforming itself into a gas-based economy, the journey has just begun. We are still nowhere close to the 15 per cent share mark. It would, therefore, be prudent to also look critically at the many other benefits that could accrue to us from a gas-based economy—these are the things that are perhaps needed in the next phase as we seek to decarbonize India through the gas route.

Certain sectors of our economy are still not able to derive the full advantage of natural gas, largely due to the lack of accessibility. I am convinced that steel is one such sector. Senior steel industry representatives have told me that gas-fired steel units are capable of manufacturing high-grade steel, which is presently imported. The states of Jharkhand, Odisha, West Bengal and Chhattisgarh, which are going to get connected with the NGG in the next couple of years have abundant iron ore mines as well as large steel units in the public and private sectors. Availability of competitively-priced natural gas to these units can transform the Indian steel industry.

Likewise, power generation is another sector where India can push for higher utilization of natural gas. Over the last three years, approximately 30 mmscmd gas was consumed by gas-based power plants. Notwithstanding this, more than half of India's approximately 27 GW installed capacity of gas-based plants is either stranded or not operating at economic levels due to shortage of affordable natural gas. Under the Conference of Parties (CoP)-21 Paris Accord, India has pledged to generate 40 per cent power from clean sources by 2030. In June 2018, India scaled up its renewable energy generation capacity target from the earlier 175 GW to 227 GW. Going forward, renewable sources are ever more likely to become the mainstay for meeting power demand. That said, since power from renewables is often intermittent, it may be more prudent and environment friendly to use gas-fired power plants, instead of coal-based thermal plants, as spinning reserve to meet peaking power demand. Alternatively, the government may consider mandating a certain portion of power purchased by the distribution companies (DISCOMs) to be from gas-fired plants on similar lines as the Renewable Power Purchase Obligation. In either case, there is a need to build consensus in the matter.

> India has pledged to generate 40 per cent power from clean sources by 2030.

Some portion of our domestic gas invariably goes un-monetized as a result of either unavoidable flaring due to technical constraints in certain oilfields or stranding owing to lack of infrastructure or marketability. The Oil and Natural Gas Corporation Ltd (ONGC) reported flaring of gas to the tune of 1.9 per cent during 2017-18, which, to its credit, is an improvement over the 2.4 per cent reported the previous year. A resource-scarce country like India can ill afford such losses. While such losses can't be eliminated altogether, the gas industry needs to deliberate more on this and find a way to minimize these.

CONCLUSION

Decarbonizing India through increased adoption of natural gas is certainly the way forward but this could well be a long journey involving costly trade-offs. There is a need to cultivate a constituency across social and political divides to ensure that the buy-in for natural gas doesn't get diluted or compromised. Moreover, climate finance is emerging as a powerful discipline in its own right. At the recently concluded CoP24 climate talks in Katowice in Poland, the World Bank pledged to double its investments for combating threats from climate change to $200 billion for the period 2021–25. We must make sure that projects promoting natural gas usage get their rightful support from the fraternity of financial institutions. Finally, we can build and sustain a vibrant gas-based economy in India only if we have competent human capital for this—all industry participants need to come together to develop the requisite skill sets in our people.

6

REFORMS IN THE OIL AND GAS SECTOR

Adil Zainulbhai

India is the fastest growing large economy in the world now. It is already the sixth largest economy with a GDP of $2.6 trillion. To fuel this speed of development, India consumed 212 million tonnes (mt) of oil products in 2017, coming behind only China (554 mt) and the US (773 mt). However, at a per capita level, India's household energy consumption, 0.7 tonne of oil equivalent in 2017, is far behind that in many other developing countries (for example, China's was 2.2 tonnes). As the economy develops and more people improve their living standards, our energy demand will increase rapidly. Therefore, it is not surprising that India's energy consumption is expected to grow at the fastest rate among all the major economies. India will overtake China as the largest growth market in 2020. Oil and gas together constitute 35 per cent of India's primary energy basket, but India is heavily dependent on imports for meeting its need. India imports nearly 80 per cent of its oil requirement and 45 per cent of its gas requirement. Crude oil and petroleum products, which accounted for 23 per cent of the total dollar value of imports in 2017–18, is by far the largest line item in India's import bill and therefore, intricately connected to the health of the Indian economy. All of this drives home the importance of a well-planned energy policy.

The key priorities of India's energy policy should be four-fold. First: *Making India energy independent to a greater degree.* For a heavily import dependent country like ours, the importance of energy security cannot be exaggerated. Many reforms have been introduced to increase the domestic production of hydrocarbons and long-standing import agreements have been secured with other countries to ensure a steady supply of fuel for India's future needs. Second: *Moving towards cleaner fuels.* Some of the most radical reforms over the past few years have been focused on transforming India into a cleaner gas economy, be it through city gas distribution (CGD) or the trading hub. The regulations regarding automotive fuel quality have been upgraded. Third: *Improving access to fuels for all Indians.* The distribution network for oil and gas has been made more expansive through pipelines and retail outlet expansion and the bottom of the pyramid has been empowered with affordable access to clean cooking fuel through the Ujjwala scheme. Fourth: *Removing legacy inefficiencies.* Many old and inefficient systems such as diesel price regulation and fortnightly price revisions were removed and others like the New Exploration and Licensing Policy (NELP) have been replaced with more robust frameworks like the Hydrocarbon Exploration and Licensing Policy (HELP). These watershed reforms in India's energy policy have put it on the right track towards achieving availability, accessibility, affordability and sustainability of energy usage.

REMOVING LEGACY INEFFICIENCIES

Many features of our energy policy were conceptualized at a time of control and regulation. As we have opened up our markets and realized the benefits of free competition, some of these features become redundant or counterproductive. We have seen bold initiatives in the recent past to reform such policies.

> India's energy consumption is expected to grow at the fastest rate among all the major economies. India will overtake China as the largest growth market in 2020.

Diesel price deregulation decreased subsidy burden and improved the profitability of OMCs

Diesel accounted for 45 per cent of total under-recoveries from public sector oil marketing companies (OMCs) in 2013–14. Even though the government bore a major share of under-recoveries, the working capital was affected due to uncertain timing and the amount of disbursement. After deregulation in October 2014, the OMCs came to a position from where they could better control their finances. It contributed to improving the profitability of public sector OMCs, which had lower gross refining margins as compared to private sector competitors such as Reliance or Essar. As a result, they were able to invest in adding new downstream capacity. Furthermore, private refiners who were exporting their diesel due to subsidized market rates started selling in the domestic market. Apart from all this, the petroleum subsidy burden, which used to be ₹96,000 crore in 2012, has dropped to ₹25,000 crore in 2018.

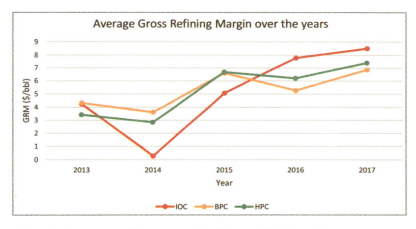

Figure 1: Average gross refining margin of public sector OMCs over the years

Source: http://petroleum.nic.in/more/indian-png-statistics (accessed on 15 January 2019)

Daily pricing benefited both our companies and consumers

Indian Oil Corporation Limited (IOCL), Hindustan Petroleum Corporation Limited (HPCL) and Bharat Petroleum Corporation Limited (BPCL) have implemented daily revision of the retail selling price of petrol and diesel in the entire country effective 16 June 2017, replacing the earlier system of fortnightly price revision. Daily pricing brought more transparency and improved logistics management and efficiency in pricing. It ensured that the benefit of even the smallest of changes in international oil prices is passed down to dealers and end users every day. Earlier, in the event of a sharp fluctuation in prices, price shocks were transferred to either the suppliers or the buyers and were maintained for at least a fortnight before being revised to reflect the latest prices. Now, the benefit of declining crude prices will be passed on to the customer the next day itself. Similarly, the benefit of a rise in crude prices will be immediately passed on to the OMCs. It has suppressed speculative activities in the market and minimized the impact on the working capital of companies and dealers.

BUILDING A GAS ECONOMY

Natural gas accounts for 6.2 per cent of our energy basket compared to the global average of 24 per cent. India's natural gas market has been historically ridden with price regulation and preordained allocation. This has led to a distorted market devoid of the genuine price signals necessary for a free market to thrive. As a result, the sector has suffered from a lack of investor interest. In 2016, the Prime Minister announced the target of achieving 15 per cent gas share in the energy basket. As a part of the project, the government has driven many gas-related reforms across markets, transmission infrastructure and affordability.

Operationalizing a gas trading hub will help in market-based price discovery

The Petroleum and Natural Gas Regulatory Board (PNGRB) has been spearheading the formation of India's maiden gas trading hub, which will help suppliers and buyers discover the price of gas and ensure efficient allocation. This is in contrast to the status quo, where the government allocates the majority of local production to high-priority sectors at prices determined by prices in gas-surplus nations—the US, Canada, Russia and the UK. As a result, locally produced gas is available at $3.06 per British thermal unit whereas imported liquefied natural gas (LNG) is available at upward of $7.5. The trading hub will help bridge this gap slowly. The unbundling of the transmission and marketing divisions of GAIL, the largest pipeline provider in the country, is another pivotal step towards achieving a mature gas economy in India. As a step in the direction of enhancing transparency of the system, the government launched a portal for booking common carrier capacity in the national pipeline network for a period of less than one year. This will not only improve the utilization of the country's pipeline network—which is at 40 per cent currently—but will also enable various entities to procure natural gas in a transparent and cost-effective manner through a digital interface.

The PM Urja Ganga scheme is bringing eastern and north eastern India on to the gas pipeline grid

Till recently, the natural gas grid connected the gas sources majorly to the western, south-eastern and northern areas, while the eastern regions remained off the grid. Under the PM Urja Ganga scheme, 3,376 km of pipeline is being built to connect six states—UP, Bihar, Jharkhand, West Bengal, Odisha and Assam—with the national grid so that these states can also get the benefits of natural gas. Further, 1,500 km of pipeline is also being built in the seven sister states of Northeast India. The pipelines will not only ensure supply of piped natural gas (PNG) for cooking and compressed natural gas (CNG) for vehicles, but will also ensure uninterrupted supply of gas to industries where it is used as a fuel or a feedstock, like power, steel, fertilizers, etc.

CGD is bringing cheap, clean fuel to 70 per cent of the Indian population

The CGD project has received unprecedented impetus in the past five years. In April 2018, the PNGRB made bidding attractive for companies by extending the marketing exclusivity period to eight years from the previous five years. At the same time, it provided greater weightage to the number of CNG stations and PNG connections guaranteeing maximum expansion of the gas network in the interest of consumers. Gas sector companies have bid for 143 geographical areas and 221 districts within the past five years, bringing in an investment of ₹70,000 crore. As per the commitment made by various entities in the ninth bidding round, around two crore PNG (domestic) connections and 4,600 CNG (transport) stations are expected to be installed in the next eight years across the country. Additionally, fifty new geographical areas, covering 124 districts in fourteen states, are expected to be covered by the end of the tenth CGD bidding round. This will increase the coverage to nearly 53 per cent of the country's area and 70 per cent of the population. CNG is cheaper than petrol and diesel and PNG is cheaper than LPG. Expansion of the gas grid will incentivize local populations to shift to natural gas as transport fuel and cooking fuel. This will free up more subsidized LPG cylinders from cities to be redirected towards the rural population, and lower emissions will provide health benefits.

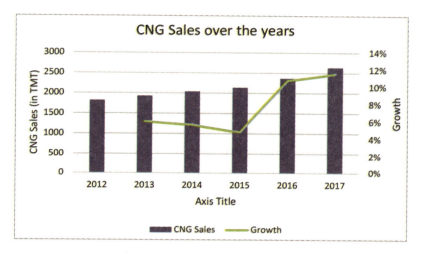

Figure 2: CNG Sales over the years

Source: *http://petroleum.nic.in/more/indian-png-statistics (accessed on 15 January 2019)*

Renegotiated LNG import agreements provide cheap gas while saving ₹25,000 crore

India imports nearly half of its gas requirement in the form of LNG, making it the fourth largest importer. To ensure long-term stable and diversified supply to fulfil its goal of transforming to a gas economy, India has entered into long-term import agreements with Qatar (saving ₹10,000 crore), Russia (saving ₹9,000 crore), Australia (saving ₹4,000 crore) and USA over the past few years. LNG import capacity, which stands at 28 mt, has increased by 23 per cent in the past four years and is expected to double over the next two years with the opening of new import terminals on the east and west coasts as well as in other countries. In addition to these, the government has halved customs duty on imported LNG to make it cheaper.

The Ujjwala scheme provided six crore LPG connections to below poverty line (BPL) families free of cost

According to the 2011 census, 85 per cent of rural households and 25 per cent of city households used some form of biomass, coal or kerosene as cooking fuel. The exposure to smoke is known to cause ailments such as pneumonia in young children and lung disease, heart disease, strokes and lung cancer in adults. Launched in 2016, the Pradhan Mantri Ujjwala Yojana (PMUY) has distributed six crore deposit-free LPG connections to such BPL households by the end of 2018. LPG coverage now extends to almost 90 per cent of the population, from 54 per cent in 2014; 48 per cent of the beneficiaries are scheduled castes or tribes scheduled castes/scheduled tribe (SC/STs). In addition to making clean energy accessible and affordable for backward sections of society, Ujjwala has also significantly contributed in improving the health of the most vulnerable sections of BPL households—women and children. Besides providing leisure to womenfolk, the scheme has empowered them financially, since a Jan-Dhan account in the name of a female family member is mandatory for an LPG connection. As a result, women have bank accounts in their name with ready deposit of subsidies. The annual average demand for LPG cylinder refills is now three, under PMUY. Nearly 80 per cent of the beneficiaries return for an average of four refills. In the process of increasing coverage, the scheme has also increased employment by expanding 13,896 dealerships in 2014 to 20,227 in 2018. An additional 3,750 distributorships have been commissioned in 2018–19.

Ujjwala has also significantly contributed in improving the health of the most vulnerable sections of BPL households— women and children.

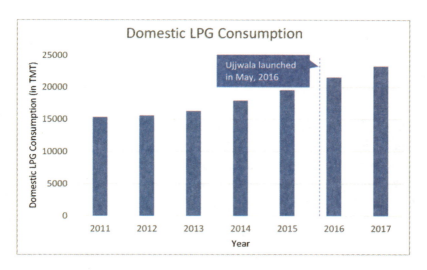

Figure 3: Domestic LPG Consumption over the years

Source: *http://petroleum.nic.in/more/indian-png-statistics (accessed on 15 January 2019)*

A strong community-based information, education and communication campaign is the final piece in the success of the massive welfare programme that is Ujjwala. Tens of thousands of LPG panchayats have played an important role in increasing community awareness about the benefits of using LPG over traditional polluting fuels like wood. The panchayats generate useful on-ground feedback from the beneficiaries about how to make Ujjwala better. Ultimately, they have helped build a common knowledge base by increasing interaction among all the stakeholders for creating a movement around Ujjwala, which ensures sustained use of LPG.

Direct benefits transfer of LPG plugged leakages worth ₹50,000 crores

The direct benefits transfer of LPG (DBTL) model called the 'PAHAL' led to a total savings of ₹50,000 crores through a targeted subsidy delivery programme. Households with taxable income less than ₹10 lakhs can provide their Aadhaar number or bank account details (in case of absence of Aadhaar) to receive subsidy directly in their accounts. PAHAL has helped in flagging 'ghost' or multiple accounts and inactive accounts. Having transferred ₹96,625 crore directly into the bank accounts of consumers, PAHAL set the Guinness record for being the largest DBT scheme. Diversion of subsidized LPG to commercial purposes has been curbed as a result of this reform.

Unique 'Give It Up' scheme inspired 1.04 crore families to transfer their subsidies to the poor

Under the 'Give It Up' scheme, the Prime Minister urged well-to-do households to voluntarily give up their LPG subsidies so that they could be transferred to the poor who rely on polluting cooking fuels such as wood, dung, crop residues and coal. The Prime Minister also called upon business houses and banks to encourage their employees to give up the subsidy on LPG, and the scheme was presented as a nation-building exercise. The procedure to give up LPG subsidy was made extremely easy. Customers could give up their subsidy online, through a text message or a mobile app, or at the local gas agency. Around 1.04 crore connections responded to the Prime Minister's call and gave up their LPG subsidy voluntarily. According to conservative estimates, IOCL, BPCL and HPCL collectively raked in nearly ₹1,280 crores in 2017-18 through the 'Give it Up' campaign.

INCREASING AVAILABILITY OF FUEL: IMPROVING THE EXPLORATION, PRODUCTION AND MARKETING SECTORS

India imports 80 per cent of its oil requirement, and its domestic oil production has also fallen continuously for six years in a row. This fall can be attributed to the lack of efficient production and drilling from matured oil fields. Soaring crude prices in the early part of the 2010s was a big reason for a lot of investment in upstream activity across the globe. Fresh investments into oil fields were rare post 2015, as low crude oil prices rendered them unattractive. Similarly, the gas pricing formula left the gas price at a level that made gas exploration and production uneconomical. Nonetheless, the rules governing upstream activity in India had many weaknesses, which were done away with in recent years in favour of a more robust and investor-friendly energy regime.

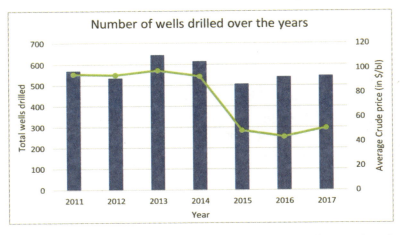

Figure 4: Number of wells (exploratory and development) drilled over the years, alongside average crude price

Source: *http://petroleum.nic.in/more/indian-png-statistics (accessed on 15 January 2019)*

HELP has made the licensing of hydrocarbons simple, transparent and less cumbersome:

To deal with these issues, the government came out with the comprehensive HELP to make exploration more transparent and less cumbersome. The policy created a uniform licence for all forms of hydrocarbons—conventional and unconventional oil and gas resources like coal-bed methane (CBM), shale gas/oil, tight gas and gas hydrates—under a single licence. There were separate policy regimes for conventional oil and gas, coal-bed methane, shale oil, and gas and gas hydrates in NELP, the previous exploration regime.

OALP will accelerate exploration activity by simplifying the acreage allotment process

According to estimates, India has exploited only 3 per cent of its proven natural gas reserves and around 5 per cent of its proven oil reserves. Out of its total sedimentary area of 3.14 million square km, 48 per cent was unapprised till 2013. To encourage exploration activity, the Open Acreage Licensing Policy (OALP) was instituted under HELP to enable fast survey and coverage of the unexplored geographical area of the country. Earlier, exploration was determined by the blocks which were put on auction by the government. There were situations where exploration companies themselves had information or interest regarding other areas where they would like to pursue exploration. These opportunities remained untapped until the government brought them to bidding at some stage in NELP. Now any exploration and production (E&P) entity can submit their expression of interest (EOI), in response to which the government will call competitive bids and assign the block for exploration activity.

Pricing freedom will make otherwise unviable projects feasible

Besides, the E&P companies have been provided freedom to market and price the gas produced by them in difficult terrains such as high pressure, high-temperature (HPHTs) reservoirs and deep water and ultra-deep water areas, which are associated with high costs and high risks. This reform was implemented to improve the viability of discoveries already made and monetize future discoveries. To protect the interest of consumers, a ceiling was introduced based on the landed price of alternative fuels. The regulated prices of domestically produced gas constitute almost half the market rate of imported LNG. It makes sense to deregulate prices sooner or later to make domestic production viable. The move was expected to monetize 160 bcm of reserves—worth $28.35 billion, assuming a production profile of fifteen years.

Revenue Sharing Contracts remove the need for the government to micro-monitor projects

For cases of successful discovery of commercial reserves, the previous profit sharing contracts have been replaced with revenue sharing contracts. Since earlier profit sharing contracts provided the government a share of the profits of the private contractor after cost recovery, the government was forced to closely monitor the work and finances of the companies to prevent manipulation by contractors to reduce the government's share of the profits. This led to interference and slow decision- making. Under the new regime, the government will not be concerned with the cost incurred and will receive a share of the gross revenue from the sale of oil, gas, etc.

DSF policy will help in early monetization of idle oil and gas fields

The Discovered Small Fields Policy (DSF) was introduced in 2016 with the motive of extracting the oil and natural gas from the un-monetized small oil and gas discoveries that are available under Oil and Natural Gas Corporation Limited (ONGC) and Oil India Limited (OIL). It offered incentives like pricing freedom and lower taxes, as well as exemption from oil cess and customs duty on items imported for operations.

Investments above ₹120,000 crore have been committed under the HELP regime

In October 2018, ₹60,000 crore of investment in exploration was committed in the latest OALP-1 round with the awarding of fifty-five oil and gas blocks. These fifty-five fields represent a total area of 59,000 square km, as against the 102,000 square km of area that is currently under exploration. Before this, in 2016, 776 square km of area was awarded under the Discovered Small Fields-1 round, bringing in an investment of ₹4,000 crore.

The bidding for 3,042 square km of area is under way as a part of DSF Round 2. Under OALP-2, fourteen blocks covering 29,333 square km are expected to bring in investments of ₹40,000 crore.

Developments in data infrastructure will complement accelerated exploration activity

To boost India's oil and gas production in the face of a flattening production curve, the government instituted the National Seismic Program for Unapprised Fields. The programme aims to undertake a fresh appraisal in all sedimentary basins across India, especially where scanty data is available, to have a better understanding of the hydrocarbon potential of India. ONGC and OIL have been asked to conduct 2D seismic acquisition, processing and interpretation (API) across India by March 2019. To aid the exploration activity, the government has set up the nation's first National Data Repository (NDR) for providing crucial hydrocarbons-related geoscientific data from sedimentary basins all over India's. By storing, maintaining and reproducing reliable data, readily accessible to players of the E&P sector, the repository will encourage new exploration activity. It will also improve the efficiency of the Directorate General of Hydrocarbons' capability to monitor and control the E&P activities in the country.

Investment in ER Technology will produce an additional 120 mmt oil in twenty years

To boost the production from fields with flattening or declining output, the government has launched a policy framework to promote enhanced recovery (ER) methods for oil and gas. The government has launched a set of initiatives to build a network of supportive knowledge systems and skilled personnel, which are needed to implement ER projects. The plan is to assess all fields from the viewpoint of ER projects and identify compatible ER methods and an attractive financial model with incentives for the contractors to undertake the project. Financial incentives include partial waiver of cess/royalty on the additional production as a result of the implementation of ER techniques for a 120-month period, starting from the date of commercial production. ER methods are expected to add an additional 120 mmt of oil and an additional 52 bcm of gas to India's production over the next twenty years, advancing India towards its goal of reducing import dependence.

Global oil interests and SPRs are steps towards energy security

Indian OMCs have acquired oil and gas resources across the globe over the past few years. Oil companies have acquired stakes in Abu Dhabi's Lower Zakum oil field and Oman's Mukhaizna oil field. ONGC Videsh acquired a 15 per cent stake in Vankorneft. The consortium of OIL, IOCL and Bharat PetroResources Limited (BPRL) acquired a 23.9 per cent stake in Vankorneft and a 29.9 per cent stake in Taas-Yuryakh, the Siberian oil field. These acquisitions strengthen India's position from the viewpoint of energy security. Additionally, 5.3 mmt of strategic petroleum reserves (SPR) have been set up to provide oil in case of supply disruption. Another 6.5 mmt of SPR is slated to come up over the next phase. Abu Dhabi National Oil Company invested $400 million in India's SPR in Mangalore.

Increasing refining and petrochemicals capacity

India's oil consumption has grown at a compound annual growth rate (CAGR) of around 5.4 per cent over the past five years. Although India currently has a surplus refining capacity and exports finished petroleum products, it must still invest in increasing the refining capacity due to the rapid growth in consumption and demand of petroleum products in the country. According to an International Energy Agency (IEA) forecast this demand will reach 458 mt by 2040, whereas currently India's refining capacity is 247 mt, clearly showing the need to continuously add refining capacity year after year. Similarly, in the area of petrochemicals, India is a net importer. India's per capita consumption of polymer is only 10 kg per person—much lower than the global average of 30 kg per person. With economic growth expected in the range of CAGR 6–8 per cent over the next two decades, the demand for petrochemicals is also going to increase steeply—and to keep up with it, we need to build our petrochemical capacity. Thanks to a vibrant oil and gas regime of forward-looking reforms, India is seeing many new investments in these areas. India's refining capacity is expected to reach 438.65 mt by 2030. In the past four years, 17.5 million metric tonne per annum (mmtpa) of brownfield extension and 15 mmtpa of greenfield extension has taken place. India's first ultra-modern 9 mmtpa greenfield refinery with a petrochemical complex has been opened in Barmer, Rajasthan. A 60 mmtpa mega refinery with a 14 mmtpa petrochemical complex is being set up in Ratnagiri. It is the world's biggest greenfield refinery, with the participation of Saudi Aramco and the Abu Dhabi National Oil Company (ADNOC). A refinery was also set up in Paradip, which will also have a petrochemical complex and a textile park nearby.

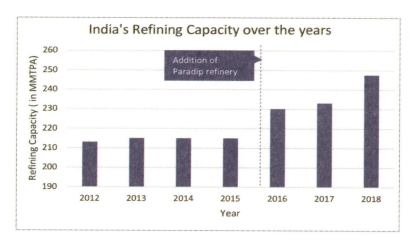

Figure 5: India's Refining Capacity over the years

Source: *http://petroleum.nic.in/more/indian-png-statistics (accessed on 15 January 2019)*

IMPROVING ACCESSIBILITY OF FUEL

The fuel distribution network has improved

The penetration of retail outlets has been steadily increasing for the past eight years. Marketing companies are in the process of launching the next phase of major retail expansion, as they announced the opening of 50,000 new retail outlets recently. Oil marketing companies have pioneered the Kisan Seva Kendras (KSKs) as low-cost retail outlets in rural areas for doorstep delivery of diesel and other petroleum products to farmers and other consumers in rural areas. The KSKs also serve as retail outlets for many other items of importance to the rural economy and lifestyle. Over 12,000 KSKs have been set up by IOCL.

ADIL ZAINULBHAI ▸

Thanks to a vibrant oil and gas regime of forward-looking reforms, India is seeing many new investments in these areas. India's refining capacity is expected to reach 438.65 million tonnes by 2030.

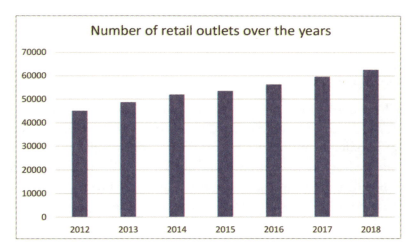

Figure 6: Number of total retail outlets over the years

Source: *http://petroleum.nic.in/more/indian-png-statistics (accessed on 15 January 2019)*

Petrol and diesel distribution has been made hassle-free

Many reforms have been introduced to improve the retail consumer's experience at the interface of retail outlets (ROs). The government has spearheaded many civic technology initiatives by means of ROs. Getting an LPG connection has been made a hassle-free experience through the online SAHAJ portal. Consumers are entitled to submit refill booking feedback on distributor services on MyLPG. in. The Ministry of Petroleum and Natural Gas (MoPNG) e-seva is functioning as a window to entertain grievances through social media. Ninety per cent ROs are equipped with infrastructure for digital payments. BPCL is piloting India's largest payment automation project at 6,500 outlets. OMCs are also exploring avenues for door-to-door delivery of petrol in their mobile dispensers. The sheer range of steps shows how various reforms, inspired by a free healthy market and regime, are ultimately expanding access to oil and gas as well as making consumers' experience seamless and safer.

Social and governance initiatives are being driven through ROs

The ministry took the help of the Quality Council of India to conduct a pan-India survey of 4,200 ROs to rank them on the basis of cleanliness during the Swachhta Pakhvada of 2018. Madurai emerged as the cleanest RO among BPCL cities and Faridabad emerged as the cleanest for both IOCL and HPCL. Such initiatives have been found to promote better performance by the entire lot through a stronger sense of competition. Of the total 56,601 PSU ROs, 55,784 have toilets. 31,381 ROs have the facility of separate toilets for men and women. The Ministry's commendable efforts in pushing the Swachhta mission was awarded in the Inter-Ministerial category in 2018's 'Swachhta Hi Seva' campaign.

CONTAINING OUR CARBON FOOTPRINT

India accounts for 6 per cent of global carbon dioxide emissions, much behind countries like China (28 per cent) and the USA

(16 per cent). However, India is one of the fastest growing energy markets and sustainability should be a fundamental principle in taking all energy policy-related decisions. Therefore, India was one of the early entrants to the Paris Agreement, committing to reduce its share of fossil fuels. India is well on its way towards achieving its goal, as we see renewables becoming more and more economical and popular. Apart from pushing the gas economy in a big way, many other oil and gas sector reforms also stand India in good stead in achieving its Sustainable Development Goals (SDGs).

The National Biofuel Policy will increase ethanol production, help farmers and control pollution

In an initiative to reduce India's oil dependence and to improve carbon footprint, the government is promoting biofuel usage in the country. Currently, the OMCs are chasing the target of 5 per cent ethanol blend. India has the target of 10 per cent blend by 2022. After releasing the National Biofuel Policy in 2018, the Prime Minister has indicated that India can aspire to achieve 20 per cent blend by 2030. As things stand, the sugarcane available is sufficient for achieving less than 3.5 per cent blend. The reasons behind inadequate supply are uneven distribution of sugarcane production, fluctuating supply due to seasonality, poor transport and storage infrastructure and higher prices provided by the liquor sector. Just sugarcane is not enough to meet India's ambitious ethanol-blending target.

Therefore, the National Biofuel Policy allowed the use of sugarcane juice, sugar containing materials (sugar beet, sweet sorghum), starch containing materials (cassava, corn), damaged foodgrains (broken rice, rotten potato) and crop residue (wheat and rice stubble) as feedstock in the production of ethanol. It is essential to commission second-generation biorefiners which can produce ethanol from agricultural residue. These 2G biorefiners have tremendous potential of solving the annual pollution problem of North India by preventing straw burning at the end of the kharif season. The government and central public sector oil companies have planned to set up twelve 2G biorefiners with an overall outlay of ₹10,000 crores and a projected annual production of 35 to 40 litres of ethanol in eleven states: Punjab, Haryana, Madhya Pradesh, Bihar, Assam, Odisha, Gujarat, Maharashtra, Karnataka and Andhra Pradesh.

The government has also announced that the OMCs will procure ethanol derived from B-heavy molasses, or 100 per cent sugarcane juice at a 25 per cent higher price than before. This move by the OMCs will help attract sellers towards the ethanol-blended-petrol (EBP) market instead of the liquor market. In addition to that, the increased prices and purchase by OMCs will increase the liquidity of sugar mills, which will in turn help clear farmer arrears.

5,000 CBG plants will produce fuel from waste, reducing import dependence

Another initiative based on generating fuel from waste is Sustainable Alternative Towards Affordable Transportation (SATAT). The scheme aims to benefit both farmers and the automobile sector by promoting the setting up of compressed biogas (CBG) plants that will produce CBG from biomass waste such as agricultural residue, municipal solid waste, sewage treatment plant waste, distillery spent wash, sugarcane waste mud, rotten potatoes from cold storage, treated organic waste from effluent treatment plants, etc. CBG comes within the category of advanced biofuels, which are being promoted under the National Biofuel Policy. CBG, which is exactly similar to CNG, can complement CNG across the gas stations of the country. Over time, it can be integrated into the CGD network for distribution to domestic as well as transport sector users. It will not only reduce import dependence for oil and gas, it will also provide a fantastic avenue for India's solid waste management system and a potential relief from the pollution caused by stubble burning. Under SATAT, the government is incentivizing private entrepreneurs to set up 5,000 CBG plants over the next five years.

Tighter automotive fuel regulation will clamp vehicular pollution

The global climate agreements are a major factor determining the energy policies of countries around the world. The Government of India implemented the Bharat Stage (BS) IV standard in 2017 and announced that the BS VI will be applicable from 2020 instead of 2024. This leap from BS IV to BS VI significantly curtails sulphur and nitrogen oxide levels in emission. In general, it will reduce pollution from diesel vehicles by 80 per cent. BS VI will also mandate the addition of an on-board diagnostics device to inform the user of the efficiency of the vehicle's fuel consumption system and flag any malfunction that may lead to a rise in emissions above permissible levels.

Some of these measures have had immediate impact like Ujjwala, whereas others like HELP, which are more structural in nature, will deliver results in due time. Irrespective of that, all these reforms have been long awaited and implementing them now, replacing years- or decades-old norms with conviction, is commendable. Energy has become more accessible, more affordable and cleaner for India's people. We are on our way towards creating an efficient energy market for our industries—and steadily, we will get there.

7

COAL IN INDIA'S ECONOMY: AN AGENDA FOR REFORMS

Arvind Panagariya and *Anil Jain*

For an ancient civilization such as India, the history of coal mining is of remarkably recent origin. D.P. Jha of the Indian School of Mines in Dhanbad states that there is no definite Sanskrit word for mined coal. Kautilya's *Arthashastra* is also silent on it despite its extensive references to mining of other minerals. Indian tribes such as the Lohar are known to have smelted iron since ancient times, but they did this with charcoal, produced from slow burning of wood (Jha 1982). The history of coal in India is, therefore, less than two and a half centuries old.

The beginning of coal mining in India may be traced to 1774, when two Britons first ventured to mine it in Raniganj in modern-day West Bengal. Significant production of the mineral did not begin, however, until the arrival of steam locomotives in 1853. Annual production around this time rose to 1 million tonne. By 1900, it rose to 6.1 million tonnes and by 1920 to 18 million tonnes. In 1946, production stood at 30 million tonnes.[1]

---

[1] This and the following three paragraphs are based on Government of India data (2017).

At Independence, railways in the public sector and several private players owned coal mines in India. In 1956, the Government of India set up the National Coal Development Corporation (NCDC), which took charge of the collieries owned by the railways. The same year, the government of Andhra Pradesh took control of the Singareni Collieries Company Limited (SCCL), which had operated as a private company since 1945. Later, the Government of India acquired a 49 per cent stake in SCCL.

Although coal production saw a more steady growth in the post-Independence era, it still grew at a relatively slow pace in the early decades reflecting slow growth of the economy. In 1971–72, countrywide coal production stood at 76 million tonnes. At this time, the country was in the grip of a nationalization wave unleashed by the then Prime Minister Indira Gandhi. Major banks and the insurance sector had already been nationalized, and it was now the turn of coal. The process was completed in two phases. In the first phase, coking coal alone was nationalized while in the second phase both coking and non-coking coal became captive to the public sector (with minor exceptions).

The Coking Coal Mines (Emergency Provisions) Act, 1971, enacted in October 1971, allowed the government to take over the management of coking coal mines and coke oven plants pending nationalization. The Coking Coal Mines (Nationalisation) Act, 1972 followed close on its heels. This act nationalized all 214 coking-coal mines and twelve coke oven plants in the private sector, excluding those held by Tata Iron & Steel Company Limited (TISCO) and Indian Iron & Steel Company Limited (IISCO). In the second phase, two additional acts, Coal Mines (Taking Over of Management) Act, 1973, and Coal Mines (Nationalisation) Act, 1973, gave the government ownership of both coking and non-coking coal mines.

In the following decades, coal production expanded more rapidly than during the first quarter-century following Independence. It rose to 131 million tonnes in 1981–82, 249 million tonnes in 1991–92, 353 million tonnes in 2001–02, and 583 million tonnes in 2011–12 (Sreenivas and Bhosale, 2013). In 2017–18, the latest year for which we have data, India produced 700 million tonnes of coal.

Today, Coal India Limited (CIL) is the holding company of nine subsidiaries. One of these subsidiaries is located in Mozambique and pursues coal mining opportunities in that country. Of the remaining eight, seven subsidiaries produce coal while the remaining one provides exploration, planning and technical support to the production subsidiaries. CIL accounts for approximately 84 per cent of the country's total coal production. The remainder comes from captive producers, SCCL, and a few small private producers.

Indian coal and lignite reserves have been categorized into proved, indicated and inferred categories, and as on 1 April 2012, the cumulative proved reserves were 118.15 billion tonnes—including lignite reserves amounting to 6.18 billion tonnes (Government of India 2013, Table 14.23). These reserves are estimated to be about 10 per cent of the world's total reserves.[2] India has large reserves of steam coal but these have high ash content—amounting to approximately 40 per cent—while also having low calorific value. India has poor reserves of coking coal, which has meant regular imports to meet the requirements of the steel industry.

In light of its large overall reserve position, it is surprising that India is not a coal exporter. On the contrary, domestic production often falls short of meeting even domestic demand with imports

---

[2] Some commentators argue that as India has still not reported its coal reserves as per the widely accepted United Nations Framework Classification (UNFC), these numbers give false comfort. Experience of applying the UNFC on different ores in several countries has resulted in downward revisions.

filling the gap. Occasionally, India has exported small amounts of coal, but post-1979, imports have consistently outstripped them (Koizumi, Maekawa, Yudate and Inada 2006). While exports have generally hovered around the 1 million tonne mark, imports, which principally include steam coal, have skyrocketed in recent years. They stood at 215 million tonnes in 2014–15, 207 million tonnes in 2015–16, 195 million tonnes in 2016–17, and 213 million tonnes in 2017–18 (Dash 2018). Indian policymakers have been much concerned that despite large reserves, India has been unable to achieve self-sufficiency in coal. There have been ambitious announcements of large production targets but success has eluded the country so far.

KING COAL

Coal has dominated as a source of energy far more heavily in India than the rest of the world. In 1965, coal's share in the total primary energy of the world was 38 per cent. In India, this share was at a high of 67 per cent (British Petroleum 2018). These shares fell to 28 and 57 per cent, respectively, in 2016. The large reserves and inherent ease of using coal without much processing, unlike several other energy minerals, has partly contributed to its sustained high share. However, it is now on a downslide.

As the numbers below indicate, coal continues to dominate the industry but it faces challenge from newer sources such as solar and wind energy in the power sector. Here again, India's situation is different. In 2017, while globally coal accounted for 37 per cent of power generation, in India it contributed a gigantic 80 per cent share. What is notable, however, is the rising share of renewables. Between 2015 and 2017 alone, the share of renewables (wind and solar) in power in India rose by 2 percentage points. The sectorial consumption of coal is shown in the table below.

Consumption of coal by sector (2015)	
	in million tonnes
Power	547
Steel and washeries	19
Cement	247
Others	7
TOTAL	820

Source: http://indiaenergy.gov.in/edm/#coalConsumption (accessed on 15 January 2019)

Globally, gas is making inroads into industry. The *World Energy Outlook 2018* by the International Energy Agency (IEA) projects that the demand for gas in industry is likely to drive the overall share of gas in energy (IEA 2017). Gas is convenient, faces less regulatory challenges than other fuels and is cheaper than several competitors, such as liquid fuels. A burning question is whether the global story of gas in industry will unfold in India as well. To answer that, we need to understand the commercial aspects and existing policy regimes in gas versus other fuels.

In power, the policy regime has worked in favour of coal. The regime of tariff fixation in the power sector allows a fuel cost 'pass-through'. This allows coal to expand as long as it can be delivered regardless of its cost. A similar kind of support has now been extended to renewables, which are beginning to unseat coal. Appropriate amendments in the Electricity Act of 2003 have exempted renewables from the 'merit order' dispatch provisions, mandating their consumption regardless of cost.[3] Furthermore, lately, a rising share of renewables has been provided through the renewable purchase obligations (RPOs) imposed on the utilities.

---

[3]In recent years, renewables have seen a sharp decline in cost and at times have been able to deliver power at prices below those charged by thermal plants.

This has queered the pitch against coal. However, in industry there is no equivalent policy support that may dislodge coal. Coal has an advantage due to the administered price at which CIL makes it available, and also through 'coal linkages' to consumers. There is no open discovery of price, and domestic coal is even cheaper than imported coal. This has pushed coal demand to artificially high levels. It is likely that demand would substantially shrink if the forces of demand and supply determine coal prices. How the regime of administered prices and absence of markets has impacted coal policy—allocation of mines, coal pricing and pricing in downstream sectors—is discussed later in this article. Distortions in the energy markets, caused by a fuel that accounts for more than half of India's energy consumption, call for urgent policy reforms.

CHALLENGES FACING COAL

As coal is a nationalized commodity, government has full rights over affairs related to it, and has exercised the same in areas of allocation of coal mines, deployment of public sector companies in mining, issuing pricing policy and decision-making in downstream areas such as the power sector, environmental regulations and rail transportation. It has a declared public policy of not charging the scarcity value of coal so as to keep the price of power low. While there is reservation of coal for identified priority sectors, small volumes are offered to all potential buyers through open auctions. In spite of several efforts to boost production, coal imports remain high.

In 2014, the government announced the target of 1 billion tonne production from CIL by 2020, which does not seem attainable. In 2017, the production was still at 600 million tonnes. The government even tried to open up the sector to commercial mining through a Cabinet decision on 20 February 2018, but it has not been able to operationalize this thus far due to opposition by trade unions (*The Hindu* 2018). CIL is a highly profitable company with no shortage of funds. As a public sector company, it also enjoys full government backing. Therefore, it is surprising that it has not been able to ramp up production. With the growing energy needs of the country and emergence of new competitive technologies, it is important that this plentifully available resource is optimally utilized.

> In 2017, while globally coal accounted for 37 per cent of power generation, in India it contributed a gigantic 80 per cent share.

Among the challenges facing coal in India, the most prominent ones are:

- **Supply shortages:** Nearly 8 per cent of the total thermal capacity has been going unused due to shortage of coal. Imports have helped fill the gap to some degree, but not enough to allow an acceptable level of capacity utilization in the thermal plants. Imported coal is not only expensive, its volume also remains constrained by bottlenecks in port and railway infrastructure. Thermal power plants often face situations of critically low levels of coal leading to low levels of plant load factor (PLF).
- **Inefficiencies in coal production:** The coal sector is plagued

with low productivity, high cost of mining, low quality and pilferage. When these features are combined with the high content of ash in Indian coal, several users of this mineral find imported coal to be cheaper on calorific parity basis.

- **Absence of coal market:** The bureaucratic control of coal production and supply chains is reminiscent of the license-permit raj that held back the growth of the Indian economy for many decades. A new buyer of coal has a poor chance of getting coal supplies even if she is willing to pay the asking price (except in small volumes disbursed via auctions) or obtain a coal mine for captive mining. There is already a long queue of potential buyers and policy hurdles. With prices set by CIL and unfulfilled coal supply commitments under fuel supply agreements, there is no free entry for investors even in downstream industries that depend on coal.

- **Interlinked policy distortions:** The power sector has multiple policy issues that are interlinked with the coal sector. Two main concerns relate to fuel cost pass-through in the consumer power prices and merit order dispatch provisions. These two features of policy are internally contradictory, as the former breeds inefficiency and high prices whereas the latter encourages utilities to look for cheaper, alternative sources of power. To some degree, this situation has paved the way for the emergence of renewables even in situations in which coal can be more cost effective.

- **Top-down planning and potential for redundancy:** Being devoid of market cues, CIL management is driven by decisions handed down to it from the top. While the National Electricity Policy discounts any significant growth in new thermal capacity, CIL is in the process of doubling its coal production. Renewable energy is now a major challenger and the jury is already out on whether the days of coal are slowly coming to an end. This poses a serious dilemma for the coal sector: should it increase investment in new fields and technologies or wait and watch?

▸ **Slow growth in power demand:** While it is supply-side problems that are holding back the performance of the coal sector, in the medium to long run, it is important to keep the demand-side constraints in mind as well. Unless initiatives are taken to address these constraints, demand for electricity, the major user of coal, may become a binding constraint on the growth of the latter. Growth in demand for electricity has not been robust in recent years. To be sure, rising efficiency in energy consumption has restrained the demand for electricity to some degree. For instance, the LED movement alone will shave off 6 per cent of the current total demand for electricity. But this is only part of the story. Industrial and infrastructural growth in India have been well below potential. There still remains a substantial proportion of households without electricity. Moreover, a large proportion of households that do receive electricity do not have access to it 24×7. To ensure that future growth in demand for electricity and therefore coal is robust, these factors must be systematically addressed.

Globally, there is a movement against coal due to its high carbon content, which contributes to global warming. India's nationally determined contributions to the Paris Agreement, negotiated by the twenty-first Conference of Parties (COP 21) under the auspices of the United Nations Framework Convention on Climate Change (UNFCCC) envisages 40 per cent share of non-fossil fuels in power generation capacity by 2030. This commitment still leaves room for 60 per cent share of fossil fuels in power generation.

The current low per capita electricity consumption and the large growth ambition make coal a vital energy source for India in the coming years. Air-conditioning load is expected to rise nearly four to five times by 2030—possibly even more—which would create a large demand for electricity. Manufacturing growth, infrastructure building, progressive shift towards electric vehicles, rapid access to electricity to every household, and 24×7 provision of electricity will all add to electricity demand. In turn, this would require coal as an important fuel to increase electricity supply.

In the medium to long run, the demand for electricity is thus likely to be robust. At the same time, over the years, alternative, cleaner sources of energy are going to pose a serious challenge to coal. It is even possible that after two to three decades, technological change would make coal wholly uneconomical to use. Therefore, it stands to reason that we try to make the most of coal use in the next two decades, keeping in view our commitments under the Paris Agreement. This requires some major reforms in the coal sector. The draft National Energy Policy, prepared during our tenures in NITI Aayog, offers several such reforms. In the following section, we briefly discuss some of these reforms.

REFORMS TO IMPROVE EFFICIENCY AND PROMOTE GROWTH

The energy sector is characterized by large upfront investments at both ends—production and consumption. Coal production requires large investments, as do thermal power plants, which buy coal in vast volumes. For investment in thermal power plants to take place, generation companies must be assured a steady supply of coal on the one hand and long-term power purchase agreements (PPAs) at viable prices on the other. Distribution companies, which sign PPAs on the buyer side, want to be sure that the generation company would have a steady supply of coal available for it. Therefore, to attract major capital investment in thermal plants, a necessary albeit not sufficient condition is the steady availability of coal. If coal is to maintain its dominance over the next two decades, supply assurance has to be the number one area of intervention. We need to ensure that high quality coal can be supplied at competitive prices.

The following are our key recommendations to make the coal sector more efficient and competitive:

(i) **Upstream:** This area holds the key to the overall success of reforms. By effecting policy changes, large enhancements to coal availability can be achieved. We recognize the political challenge to the privatization of one or more subsidiaries of CIL. But even while maintaining public ownership of the companies, it is possible to open up coal mining to greater competition. For example, corporatizing the seven production subsidiaries of CIL into independent companies can result in substantial competition, leading to efficiency gains. Implementing the decision to allow commercial mining may provide even more competition. Another important reform would involve reviewing the legal status of ownership of coal in private lands. Just as private landowners drove the shale gas revolution in the US, if given mining rights, vast stretches of private land with coal deposits could become the source for a coal revolution in India. This reform would call for a review of the Coal Bearing Areas Act. Given that the window for intensive exploitation of coal may be no wider than two decades, it is time to bring the same reforms to this sector that oil exploration saw in the 1990s and other mining sectors saw more recently.

(ii) **Midstream:** This segment of coal business relates to coal washing, transportation and port infrastructure. The objective of reforms in this area is to attract large investments. With nearly 40 per cent ash content in Indian coal, it does not make good business sense to haul coal from the eastern coal-mining region to the west and the north. The environmental norms for coal transport and power sector emissions should be aligned to the air quality objectives. Stricter norms would nudge thermal power generation companies towards buying washed coal and pave the way for larger investments, necessary to set up washeries. For the transportation and necessary port infrastructure for imported coal, the regime needs to be investor friendly. It is generally believed that the present regime of Indian Railways, holding a stake in the joint ventures created for coal evacuation, has stifled risk and entrepreneurship. The successful experience of Krishnapatnam in Andhra Pradesh—in integrating port and rail infrastructure with thermal plants based on imported coal—needs to be replicated in other parts of the country.

(iii) **Downstream:** The upstream reforms will go hand in hand with coal allocation policies. As has been done in the petroleum sector, the government should distance itself from coal allocation and pricing. At present, there exists a maze of administered prices, with prices varying by different categories of consumers depending on the industry type (such as power and cement) and ownership type (as in private versus public entities). A similar differentiation also exists in the allocation of captive mines, which is thankfully being phased out. The coal linkage policy, which connects the electricity price to the coal price, is yet another source of distortion—which we shall discuss separately in a following section. The existence of multiple coal grades further muddies the system of administered prices. Freeing the prices and allowing them to be determined by the market will eliminate current arbitrariness in pricing and attendant inefficiencies. With environmental regulation set at appropriate levels, the market prices will internalize all environmental cost, including the disposal.

(iv) **The linkage policy:** A continuing practice from the license-permit raj era is that of the concept of pass-through, as mentioned before. Under this practice, generation companies are allowed to pass any increase in their costs resulting from higher coal prices to distribution companies, which in turn pass on the burden to the consumers. In this manner, inefficiencies of CIL are passed on to generation companies and then ultimately to the customers. Such linkage must be ended with generation companies buying coal in the open market in which different coal companies must compete. Likewise, the existing allocations (linkage) in industry must be gradually ended in the way that captive coal mines are to be terminated by 2020. The reform needs to be driven all the way into the power sector with the linkage between the electricity price and the coal price broken. The incentive to the generators to procure the cheapest coal and produce it efficiently will only come if tariff fixation is freed and the interference of regulators in the pricing of electricity is ended. The subsidy to vulnerable sections may continue through direct benefit transfer.

We recognize that these reforms cannot be adopted overnight. Many of the prescriptions require statutory changes that face serious political obstacles, especially since CIL employs a vast number of workers with strong unions. If the existing pricing terms in supply contracts are changed there may be legal challenges as well. The power and coal ministries are in a client–supplier relationship, which adds to the complexity of the task. At the same time, the recommendations are well within the reach of a determined government. Similar changes have been successfully implemented, elsewhere. For example, Prime Minister Margaret Thatcher ended public sector dominance in coal mining in the UK within a matter of years.[4] In other energy sectors like oil, gas and electricity, reforms took place in many countries. In the late twentieth century, the European Union member countries moved away from long-term power and gas sale contracts to shorter-term ones thrashed out at the marketplace. The reform eventually deepened the markets, leading to lower power prices. PPAs were done away with and now a larger share of energy is transacted at near-term prices.

Some contrarians will no doubt invoke the age-old argument that India is different—that its diversity and noisy democracy make even a small change an uphill task, let alone the major changes we have recommended. Such contentions are wrong on two counts. First, changes in other democracies are equally difficult: few thought that in the near-socialist UK of the time, a leader like Margaret Thatcher could come along and fundamentally change the orientation of the British economy. Second, India is not as immune to change as contrarians would have us believe. As late as the 1980s, the majority view was that investment and import licensing could not be ended and that telecommunications and civil aviation would forever remain public sector monopolies. Yet both forms of licensing as well as public sector monopolies disappeared under Prime Minister P.V. Narasimha Rao.

---

[4]Pearson and Watson (2012).

CONCLUSION

The potential for growth in the demand for electricity in India remains huge, in view of the large number of households that still remain without electricity, the vast number of regions that still do not receive 24×7 electricity, the expansion in consumer demand for air-conditioning, the shift to electric cars, the expansion of infrastructure and the accelerated growth in manufacturing. Coal remains potentially the cheapest fuel for electricity generation. This would seem to secure the future of coal in India.

Yet, coal will face challenges from at least three sources. First, pressures for containing carbon emissions to deal with climate change would push for a shift towards cleaner fuels, including gas. Second, technological change would make renewables progressively more competitive. And finally, enhanced energy efficiency along various dimensions will place a lid on the growth in demand for electricity.

> India's nationally determined contributions to the Paris Agreement, negotiated by the twenty-first Conference of Parties (CoP21) under the auspices of the United Nations Framework Convention on Climate Change (UNFCCC) envisages 40 per cent share of non-fossil fuels in power generation capacity by 2030.

Both technological changes and enhanced energy efficiency on a large scale would take time. Likewise, India's current obligations to contain carbon emissions under the Paris Agreement give India considerable leeway to rely on coal as a source of energy. As such, India would appear to have a window of approximately two decades to make the most of its vast coal reserves.

But even this window has its limitations on account of one important short-run factor that militates against coal: urban air quality. To ensure that electricity generation does not damage air quality, it will be necessary to locate thermal power plants away from cities and towns. Even existing thermal power plants near cities and towns need to be moved farther away or replaced by cleaner sources of electricity. This factor would tend to add to the effective cost of coal.

Therefore, if India's vast coal reserves are to contribute to the country's development rather than being left buried under the ground forever, reforms that would make the sector competitive while also containing the environmental damage by this source of energy are essential. In this regard, India must learn from its own failure in the natural gas sector. At the beginning of this millennium, this fuel was seen as a major potential source of power in India. But policy mistakes and unwillingness to carry out necessary reforms led to a failure to take advantage of the opportunity available to the country. While the present government has at last taken much-needed corrective action, it may now take some time to achieve the objectives of a gas-based economy. The recent city gas distribution (CGD) bidding rounds and revival of closed urea plants will lead to demand creation and a rise in the share of gas in power and energy systems (PES). These actions will help cap the costs of the past mistakes.

Freeing up various prices and allowing competition in energy markets can be a game-changing reform. Markets have the potential to bring large doses of capital and drive efficiencies—two vital inputs coal could profit from. As was witnessed in the process of liberalization of the natural gas sector across Europe in the late twentieth century, ushering in free markets takes time. If India could emulate the example of freeing diesel prices in the coal sector while also unleashing competition among various coal companies through corporatization of CIL subsidiaries, it may be able to attract large volumes of capital. Gradual migration from a 'command and control' regime to a regime that at least permits some competition and allows markets to arbitrage prices in different uses can go a long way towards turning coal into at least 'black silver', if not 'black gold'. Short of such reforms, coal is not only likely to remain grossly underused, but we will also fail to achieve the benefits of clean coal technologies that require substantial investment—which can come only in the presence of profitable opportunities offered by the existence of competitive markets.

> While the present government has at last taken much needed corrective action, it may now take some time to achieve the objectives of a gas-based economy.

BIBLIOGRAPHY

British Petroleum (2018). *Statistical Review of World Energy (1965–2017)*: https://www.bp.com/content/dam/bp/en/corporate/excel/energy-economics/statistical-review/bp-stats-review-2018-all-data.xlsx.

Dash, Jayati (2018). 'After Two Years of Fall, India's Coal Imports Grow 8.1 per cent in FY18', *Business Standard*, 17 May: https://www.businessstandard.com/article/economy-policy/after-two-years-of-fall-india-s-coal-imports-grow-8-1-in-fy18-118051700016_1.html

Government of India (2013). *Twelfth Five-Year Plan*, Planning Commission, <http://planningcommission.gov.in/plans/planrel/12thplan/pdf/12fyp_vol2.pdf > (accessed on 20 December 2018).

Government of India (2017). 'Coal Mining in India: The Past', Ministry of Coal: <https://coal.nic.in/content/historybackground> (accessed on 20 December 2018).

IEA (2017). 'IEA sees global gas demand rising to 2022 as US drives market transformation': <https://www.iea.org/newsroom/news/2017/july/iea-sees-global-gas-demand-rising-to-2022-as-us-drives-market-transformation.html> (accessed on 27 December 2018).

Jha, D.P. (1982). 'Science and Technology (Coal Mining) in India in Eighteenth-Nineteenth Century', *Indian Journal of History of Science* 17(2): 377–91.

Koizumi, K., K. Maekawa, K. Yudate and N. Inada (2006). 'Coal Supply and Demand Trends in India', Institute of Energy Economics, Japan: <https://eneken.ieej.or.jp/en/data/pdf/355.pdf>

Pearson, Peter and Jim Watson (2012). *UK Energy Policy 1980–2010: A History and Lessons to be Learnt*, The Parliamentary Group for Energy Studies, London: <http://sro.sussex.ac.uk/38852/1/uk-energy-policy.pdf>

Sreenivas, Ashok and Krutuja Bhosale (2013). *Black and Dirty: The Real Challenge Facing India's Coal Sector*, Prayas Energy Group, Pune.

The Hindu (2018). 'Commercial Coal Mining Opened for Private Sector,' 20 February: <https://www.thehindu.com/business/Industry /government-clears-opening-up-of-commercial-coal-mining-to-private-firms/article22806187.ece>

8

THE ROLE OF RENEWABLE ENERGY IN INDIA'S JOURNEY TOWARDS A LOW CARBON FUTURE

Debasish Mishra

Since the second industrial revolution, electricity has played an important role in the development of humankind. Although India has been an early adopter of electricity, with legislation in place since 1910, it still has some distance to travel towards electrification of all households and other potential segments of the economy.

According to the International Energy Agency (IEA), the electricity sector globally attracts more investment now than oil and gas combined. As per IEA, global electricity demand doubled between 1990 and 2016, outpacing other fuels. It is set to grow at twice the pace of energy demand as a whole over the next twenty-five years. IEA had, in fact, declared 2018 as the year of electricity.

There are several drivers for the rapid growth in electricity demand across the world. In the Organization for Economic Cooperation and Development (OECD) countries, there is an increasing trend towards electrification of transportation and heating needs, as it is deemed to be more efficient and cleaner or emission-free. In developing countries, there has been a massive focus on improving electricity access, and better lifestyles have led to increased per capita consumption. India, for instance, has completed 100 per cent electricity access to all villages in 2018, and is targeting to provide electricity access to all households by 2019. The developing countries are also experiencing a robust growth in demand for electricity due to increasing ownership of appliances such as televisions, washing machines, air conditioners, etc.

On the electricity generation side, in the early 1990s combined cycle technology made gas-based thermal generation very efficient. This coincided with gas production in the North Sea and Europe getting access to gas from Russia. In recent times, the US has become a prolific gas producer due to production of shale gas. Many countries like the UK and the US, which were primarily dependent on coal-based thermal generation, have shifted to natural gas for electricity generation. This has significantly reduced their carbon footprint. The overall share of gas in the global primary energy mix has crossed more than 24 per cent and is expected to soon cross the share of coal. However, countries like India and China have continued to depend primarily on coal as fuel for electricity generation.

According to the Central Electricity Authority (CEA), as of 31 March 2018, thermal coal has a share of 76 per cent in the total electricity supply in India. Currently, hydroelectric power contributes just 9.7 per cent of the power supply, down from 25 per cent in the mid-1990s. With environmental concerns and difficulty in project development, the share of hydro is unlikely to go up significantly in the future.

India's attempt to adapt nuclear technology for electricity generation has also taken a back seat since the Fukushima nuclear disaster. While the indigenous pressurized heavy water reactor (PHWR) programme is progressing, the imported light water reactor (LWR) programme is stuck because of suppliers' liability issues and lack of commercial viability due to high project costs. This has also slowed down progress to the third stage of the programme—using Thorium.

> India, for instance, has completed 100 per cent electricity access to all villages in 2018, and is targeting to provide electricity access to all households by 2019.

BP, in its 2014 edition of *Energy Outlook 2035*, had predicted that China and India, combined, would contribute 87 per cent of the global incremental coal demand till 2035.[1] However, due to environmental pressures and falling prices of renewables, coal consumption declined in China—from 1,969 million tonnes of oil equivalent (mtoe) in 2013 to 1,892 mtoe in 2017. Over the last ten years (2007–17), global coal demand has been flat—growing at less than 1 per cent—reflecting the global efforts to minimize the consumption of coal, and the availability of new energy technologies. It will continue to show a declining trend

---

[1] https://www.bp.com/content/dam/bp/business-sites/en/global/corporate/pdfs/energy-economics/energy-outlook/bp-energy-outlook-2014.pdf

in OECD countries and China will try to freeze, if not reduce, its consumption at the current levels. Hence, the IEA, in its latest Coal 2018 report,[2] estimates that coal demand will remain constant over the next five years.

Among all major economies in the world, India has remained the only country with increasing coal demand, and at an annual compounded growth rate of about 5 per cent over the past decade. Although India has argued for energy justice by pointing out the need to balance development and emissions control, there is an increasing realization that it is better to moderate the usage of coal in our primary energy mix for the country's good. The National Electricity Plan (NEP) 2018 thus projects no fresh investments in thermal coal-based power plants up to 2027.

India has demonstrated serious commitment towards the global climate change initiative. It took the lead in ratifying the Paris Agreement on climate change in October 2016. As part of the Intended Nationally Determined Contributions (INDCs), India has committed to reduce the emissions intensity of its GDP by 33–35 per cent from the 2005 level by 2030. One of the main strategies India is planning to adopt towards achieving this goal is having 40 per cent electricity generation capacity from non-fossil-fuel-based energy resources by 2030.

The Government of India has undertaken several strategic initiatives for meeting the targets. The ongoing initiatives in energy efficiency through programmes like the Perform, Achieve and Trade (PAT) scheme for industries and Unnat Jyoti by Affordable LEDs for All (UJALA) scheme are targeted at reducing energy requirements. According to the National Ujala dashboard,

---

[2] https://www.iea.org/newsroom/news/2018/december/global-coal-demand-set-to-remain-stable-through-2023-despite-headwinds.html

distribution of over 300 million LED bulbs has resulted in avoided peak demand of over 8,000 MW and CO_2 reduction of 33 $MTCO_2$ every year.

The government is planning to create a carbon sink of 3 billion tonnes of CO_2 equivalent through additional forest cover. Further, the government is only allowing supercritical technology for thermal coal-based power plants—for which, according to the CEA, the specific CO_2 emissions are 17 per cent lower than those of subcritical technology. Around 42 per cent of the total capacity addition from coal units in the Twelfth Five Year Plan period (2012–17) was from supercritical technology. Similarly, the government has identified over 48,000 MW of old and inefficient thermal power units for retiring.

It would not be sufficient for India to meet its CO_2 emission reduction targets for 2030 if it just focuses on demand-side responses and moves to supercritical technology for the thermal coal units. An aggressive shift towards renewable energy (RE) in the generation mix will be required to support the initiatives for reduction in CO_2 emissions and hence achieve its INDC targets. Accordingly, India has set a massive target of 175,000 MW of renewable energy (RE) capacity by 2022, which is likely to be closer to 300,000 MW by 2030. The CEA has estimated that about 268 million tonnes of CO_2 will be avoided annually by the end of financial year (FY) 2022 due to additions in RE capacities.

One of the mega trends in the energy sector in the last decade has been the falling cost of solar photovoltaic (PV) technology. The global weighted average cost of electricity of utility-scale solar PV has fallen by about 73 per cent since 2010. The solar PV tariff has, in fact, fallen to less than US 3c/kWh in many parts of the world including Dubai, Mexico, Peru, Chile, Abu Dhabi and Saudi Arabia.[3] The Indian solar PV market has also mirrored this trend, where tariff has fallen by 80 per cent from ₹15/kWh in 2010 to less than ₹3/kWh (US 4c/kWh)[4] in 2018. Located around the Tropic of Cancer, India holds huge potential for solar energy. This has led to the government accelerating the pace of capacity addition in the solar sector.

> India has demonstrated serious commitment towards the global climate change initiative. It took the lead in ratifying the Paris Agreement on climate change in October 2016.

Overall, RE capacity in India has increased from a modest 10,000 MW to 70,000 MW in the last ten years—at a rate of 20 per cent annual growth. In this time, the share of RE capacity in the overall generation capacity has increased from 8 per cent to 20 per cent. In terms of generated electricity, this corresponds to a share of 7.8 per cent from RE sources. The NEP 2018 estimates the generation share of RE to increase to 20 per cent by 2022.

---

[3] IRENA renewable energy power generation costs in 2017
[4] ₹2.44/kWh lowest tariff discovered in 2017, Solar Energy Corporation of India Limited (SECI) Bhadla solar park auction.

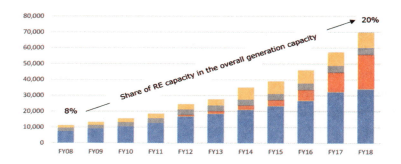

Figure 1: Renewable energy capacity addition trends (MW)
Source: Ministry of New and Renewable Energy

The existing RE capacity is around 74,000 MW, whereas the total potential is over 1,000,000 MW—giving India a huge opportunity for further development.

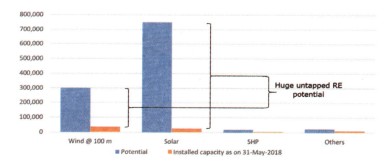

Figure 2: Renewable energy potential versus installed capacity (MW)
Source: *Ministry of New and Renewable Energy*

Considering such huge potential, its declining costs and the far-reaching implications of RE on the economy, energy security, environment and social development, India has been actively promoting this form of energy.

The massive targets set under the Renewable Energy Program and the National Solar Mission are just some of the initiatives taken by the government to spearhead the overall investment in the sector. The NEP 2018 projects no fresh investments in thermal coal-based power plants up to 2027. It estimates that the incremental demand will mostly be met by RE capacity additions. As per the NEP, the share of RE capacity is projected to increase from 20 per cent in 2018 to 37 per cent by 2022 and 45 per cent by 2027, making it the dominant technology in the overall capacity mix. Further, to accelerate the pace of RE additions, the government has released its roadmap for 2019 and 2020—to bid out 40,000 MW[5] of capacity in each of these years.

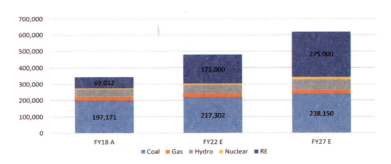

Figure 3: Generation capacity addition targets by 2022 and 2027

Sources: CEA installed capacity report and NEP 2018

In order to back the targets under these programmes, the Ministry of Power (MoP) made amendments to the National Tariff Policy (NTP) in 2016, mandating the state electricity regulatory commissions (SERCs) to revise the renewable purchase obligation (RPO) target. Following this amendment, the MoP came up with

---

[5] http://pib.nic.in/newsite/PrintRelease.aspx?relid=173830

an order in 2018 notifying SERCs to have uniform RPOs of 21 per cent by FY 2022,[6] equally distributed between solar and non-solar. To address the issue of varying RE potential across states, restricting uniform RPO, the MoP waived the interstate transmission charges and losses for solar and wind energy procured through competitive bidding.[7] The government created a RPO compliance cell in May 2018 to coordinate with SERCs and the Central Electricity Regulatory Commission (CERC) on matters relating to RPO compliance. The cell will periodically report to the government to take up non-compliance-related issues with appropriate authorities.

India has set a massive target of 175,000 MW of RE capacity by 2022.

Before 2014, the focus of the policymakers was on providing financial incentives in the form of tax benefits, feed-in tariff and generation-based incentives (GBI). Taking a cue from falling RE tariffs, RE development can be sustained without any financial support from the government, the impetus is now on reducing the development and operational risks.

The solar park scheme, announced in 2016 by the Ministry of New and Renewable Energy (MNRE), aims to reduce the

---

[6] https://powermin.nic.in/sites/default/files/webform/notices/RPO_trajectory_2019-22_Order_dated_14_June_2018.pdf

[7] https://powermin.nic.in/sites/default/files/webform/notices/Waiver_of_inter_state_transmission_of_the_electricity.pdf

development risks associated with land acquisition and other infrastructure development-related risks. The original scheme targeted parks for 20,000 MW solar power installed capacity by 2020, and it was subsequently revised to 40,000 MW solar power installed capacity by 2022 in the Union Budget for FY 2017–18.[8] Under this scheme, the solar park developer (a joint venture between a state government nodal agency and a central government nodal agency/private player) is responsible for identifying and acquiring the land, obtaining clearances, building the common infrastructure, making water available and establishing the transmission network from the park to the nearest grid substation, thereby reducing the development risk for solar project developers. To support this scheme, the MNRE provides grants of ₹25 lakh to solar park developers for preparation of the detailed project report and ₹20 lakh per MW as subsidy for developing the solar park. In addition to this financial incentive, state nodal agencies facilitate land acquisition for solar park developers.

The competitive bidding guidelines for solar and other policy impetuses have helped tap investments from several local and global investors. This has also aided in bringing the tariff down. This steep drop has been facilitated by a combination of factors like decline in module costs, increase in scale of projects, innovative project development models like solar parks, access to low-cost financing with longer repayment periods and decline in return on equity expectations due to reduced risks.

The government has periodically revised the solar bidding guidelines to address the concerns of bidders regarding development and operational issues. In the past one year, it has

---

[8] https://mnre.gov.in/file-manager/UserFiles/Scheme-for-enhancement-of-capacity-to-40GW-Solar-Parks.pdf

increased the project implementation timelines to twenty-four months from eighteen months, addressed concerns relating to transmission connectivity approvals, clarified the issue of change in rates of taxes, duties and cess; and constantly evolved the payment security mechanism by providing revolving letters of credit (LCs), creating a payment security fund and providing state government guarantees.

Competitive bidding in the wind sector was introduced only in 2017. Since then, the tariffs for wind energy too have come down by 50 per cent in less than a year. The wind tariff for the first time fell below ₹3/kWh in a Solar Energy Corporation of India (SECI) interstate transmission system (ISTS) bid allocated in October 2017. This was majorly due to advancement in wind technologies, bigger project sizes, lower capital costs and the operations and maintenance (O&M) cost offered by wind turbine generator (WTG) manufacturers, access to better financing and decline in return on equity expectations due to reduced risks, among other factors.

On the other hand, due to the increase in coal prices, the variable cost of coal-based power has shown an increasing trend of 5–6 per cent every year. In addition, the coal sector has increased the cess from ₹50 to ₹400/tonne in six years—this trend is unlikely to be reversed.

Wind and solar energy tariffs are now less than thermal tariffs in most of the large states in India. With the further projected decline in solar module prices, improvement in wind technology and lower capacity utilization of thermal power plants, the price advantage of RE over coal is expected to widen further. This is expected to drive demand for consumption of RE with utilities likely to procure more than the RPO requirement to meet their incremental demand.

Figure 4: All India tariff trends for different power generation technologies
Source: *Bid results and CERC wind FIT*

India is also looking at developing offshore wind projects. The government issued its National Offshore Wind Policy in 2015. The policy identified several challenges in terms of resource assessment and layers of clearances required from the Ministry of Defence and other ministries. It identified National Institute of Wind Energy (NIWE) as the nodal agency to coordinate with different ministries for facilitating the clearances, coordinate resource assessment and invite proposals from interested developers for implementing the projects. The government has set a target of 5,000 MW and 30,000 MW of offshore wind capacity by 2022 and 2030 respectively. The NIWE issued an expression of interest (EoI) in June 2018 inviting experienced bidders for the development of a 1,000 MW commercial offshore wind farm off the cost of Gujarat. NIWE and First Offshore Windfarm Project in India (FOWPI) have carried out several studies, including wind resource assessment, metocean measurements, wave data, tide, current, geophysical and geotechnical studies, before issuing the EoI. Around thirty-five companies have submitted their responses to this EoI.

In the last five years, India has shown significant addition in RE capacity. MNRE data shows wind capacity has increased by 1.8 times (from 18.5 GW to 34 GW) and solar by thirteen times (from 1.7 GW to 21.6 GW). However, the targets are stiff and there are several challenges in achieving them. There are challenges to integrate RE into the grid, due to intermittent generation and less predictability than the conventional sources of energy. Further, there is an additional infrastructure cost due to lower utilization of the transmission network, born of lower plant load factors than thermal power plants. The government came out with a wind-solar hybrid policy in May 2018. The policy aims to provide a framework for promotion of large grid-connected wind–solar PV hybrid systems for optimal and efficient utilization of transmission infrastructure and land, reducing the variability in renewable power generation and achieving better grid stability. The government sanctioned the first scheme for the setting up of 2,500 MW of wind–solar hybrid power projects and developed guidelines for a transparent bidding process. SECI has been identified as the nodal agency for implementation of the scheme and managing the selection process of successful developers. The first bid—for 840 MW capacity—was awarded in December 2018 with a tariff of ₹2.67 per kWh.

Battery storage has the potential for supporting RE integration initiatives, though the commercial viability of these systems is still to be established. The government, in 2017, introduced battery storage capacity as part of solar park- based bids in Karnataka and Andhra Pradesh, on a pilot basis. However, the bids have not progressed to the award stage. A few of the end-user-driven projects like NTPC Ltd's 50 MW solar project with storage facility at Port Blair,[9] and NLC India Limited's 20 MW solar project, with storage facility at Attam Pahad,[10] have shown some progress. The government is also working on several pilot projects to understand the time response and performance of the battery technologies, efficacy of the battery systems in providing grid operation support to meet regulating reserve requirements and comparing of performance of the storage systems with respect to other power system flexibility options.

Other storage options, like pumped hydroelectric, are also being evaluated. States are exploring the option of wind- and solar-pumped hydroelectric projects to provide round-the-clock clean power to utilities. However, there is a need for policy and tariff regulation to incentivize the investors' with preferential tariff to ensure adequate returns. As discussed earlier, investment in hydroelectric has shown a sharp decline over the last decade and the government is working on a new hydro policy for making these projects more attractive for investors. Some of the points that are being discussed are removing the 25 MW capacity cap[11] and classifying all sub-100 MW hydro projects as RE, introducing separate hydropower purchase obligations, providing interest subvention, and mandatory purchase of a certain quantum of hydroelectricity by the distribution companies (DISCOM).

In India, more than 90 per cent of the power capacity is contracted to utilities, while the rest is used for self-consumption or third-party sale to end consumers. Sale to utilities is likely to be the dominant business model for generators. However, with RE tariffs stabilized over the last two years, there is an increased

---

[9]https://www.ntpc.co.in/en/media/press-releases/details/ntpc-signs-mou-andaman-and-nicobar-set-50-mw-solar-power-projects-battery-energy-storage-system-port
[10]https://econts.nlcindia.com/specification/tender/1718000032
[11]https://mnre.gov.in/small-hydro

interest from industrial, commercial and residential consumers to buy RE power directly from generators or set up their own RE capacity for self-consumption. All the major states have open access and net metering regulations in place. However, there are certain regulatory uncertainties regarding long-term open access charges, continuation of energy banking provisions[12] to mention a few. The regulatory challenges seem to be restricting the potential of this business model from being fully exploited.

Although the size of the investment opportunity in the Indian renewable sector in the next decade is enormous, there are challenges that are faced by existing and potential investors. RE firms have faced impediments because of grid back-down in some states, technical unavailability of the grid and sometimes due to high system frequency.

Provision of new transmission infrastructure and integration of a large quantity of RE power into the grid in a short period remains a major challenge for the RE sector. The government was proactive in planning green energy corridors (GECs) over two phases, for evacuation of power from the regions having high enough concentration of RE to demand centres. The GECs are in the implementation process in eight RE-rich states.[13] These are being implemented in phases, with phase I covering integration of 43,000 MW and phase II of 20,000 MW. However, with the government finding it difficult to provision additional solar parks, transmission planning and development is emerging as a significant risk with all eyes on the GEC phase III programme that is under

---

[12]Most of the SERCs provided yearly energy banking a few years back, but the period has been reduced to one month banking, with some SERCs having completely withdrawn the energy banking facility.

[13]Andhra Pradesh, Gujarat, Himachal Pradesh, Karnataka, Madhya Pradesh, Maharashtra, Rajasthan and Tamil Nadu.

consideration by the government. India has adopted mandatory forecasting and scheduling for RE developers and also enabled load dispatch centres (LDCs)/system operators to centrally forecast RE, through the establishment of renewable energy management centres (REMCs). REMCs will assist LDCs in forecasting, scheduling and real-time management of renewable power as a part of the GEC scheme.

With increasing levels of RE on the grid, India's integration challenge will involve adoption of much higher levels of flexibility in the grid with introduction of supply-side flexibility (such as flexibilization of coal-based generation and optimal operation of hydro), demand-side flexibility (automatic demand-side management, for instance) and reorganization of electricity markets to enable faster reserve sharing and functional ancillary markets. Storage will inevitably play a role in balancing as RE penetration reaches much higher levels, presumably by 2027.

Fundamentally, higher levels of RE changes the paradigm of the electric grid. It requires new infrastructure (transmission corridors) provisioning, adoption of smarter and flexible grid operations, reorganized markets for reserve sharing, adequate ancillary provisions for reliability and gradual adoption of tighter interconnection standards to ensure RE generators provide the range of responses (such as system inertia, primary frequency response, etc.) that conventional generators provide today. All these will require calibrated policy and regulatory provisioning in step with the deployment of RE.

Based on the current capacity target and the ongoing capital costs for wind and solar projects, it is estimated that the entire programme for RE generation capacity addition will require significant investments of over ₹11,000 billion over the next ten years ($15 billion a year, mostly from the private sector). This is likely to be funded by debt and equity at a 75:25 ratio. On the equity side, the sector so far has received the majority of the funding from Indian corporates/promoters and private equity (PE) funds. Leading RE independent power producers (IPPs) are owned by sovereign funds, global PE funds and some Indian corporates. Recently, a few Asian sovereign funds like the General Insurance Corporation (GIC) and the Abu Dhabi Investment Authority (ADIA) and Canadian pension funds like Caisse de dépôt et placement du Québec (CDPQ) and the Canada Pension Plan Investment Board (CPPIB) have taken minority stakes in a few successful IPPs.

However, to fund the sector on such a huge scale would require more long-term equity funds from pension and sovereign wealth funds. Several domestic and international factors, like competition in the sector squeezing the returns, poor financials of utilities and investment sentiment in developed countries, have kept such investments at bay. The deals that have happened over the past two years indicate that the profile of investors has started to change. Many large RE IPPs which were originally backed by PE funds with an investment horizon of five to seven years are strategically tapping investment from long-term investors like global utilities, pension funds and sovereign wealth funds. More such deals may be required to fuel the RE programme. On the debt side, there is a temporary liquidity crunch due to lack of lending to the RE sector from public sector undertaking banks and non-banking financial companies. This is likely to be resolved in the next twelve to eighteen months.

As such, the 275,000 MW RE target would require only around 2 per cent of the land in India. Even though this quantity looks manageable, getting contiguous land parcels for developing projects that can offer economies of scale is a challenge. Some developers are not able to commission projects as per schedule owing to delays in getting land clearances, approvals and connectivity to the nearest grid point.

In the case of wind energy, most of the high potential sites are taken up by existing projects. These sites have low rating turbines (kW to 1 MW scale turbines) and hence, these projects are not able to tap the full potential of such sites. India is yet to come out with a policy with respect to repowering.

Globally, the solar industry has benefited from cheaper PV modules from China and Taiwan. The Indian RE programme has also majorly benefited from imports of this solar equipment, with around 90 per cent of the solar modules used in India being imported. The government, in July 2018, notified a 25 per cent safeguard duty on imported solar panels in a bid to promote domestic manufacturing under the 'Make in India' programme. The industry estimates that there is a tariff impact of around ₹0.3–0.35/kWh due to the imposition of safeguard duty. Although the tariff impact is allowed as a pass-through in the power purchase agreements (PPAs) for projects awarded before this notification which are under execution, there are uncertainties around the methodology for calculating this impact and the compensation mechanism.

The biggest concern that investors have is the financial health of the distribution utilities in India. More than 90 per cent of the distribution utilities in India are owned by state governments. Many of these utilities have poor financials. Also, there is a history of delayed payments to generators. The Ujwal Discom Assurance Yojana (UDAY) (one-time debt restructuring and turnaround), launched by the government in 2015 to improve the financial health and operational efficiency of utilities, has helped in easing liquidity in the short term. However, without operational improvements and tariffs truly reflecting costs, these utilities might again go back to making losses, or not make a turnaround as per plan.

The government has tried to fix the issue of delayed payments on the part of utilities by bringing in intermediaries (with good credit ratings) like SECI and NTPC that buy power from generators and further sell it to DISCOMs through back-to-back PPAs. However, the ultimate payment comes from utilities and delay in payment from them for such large RE capacities is likely to impact/burden SECI and NTPC in honouring timely payments.

India's energy future, as enunciated by Prime Minister Narendra Modi, has four pillars—energy access, energy efficiency, energy sustainability and energy security. Overall, for each one of these targets to be met, India will have to get its RE programme right.

Further, the sector also has potential to generate substantial employment over its life cycle. The Ministry of Skill Development and Entrepreneurship created the Skill Council for Green Jobs under the National Skill Development Mission. The Council aims to identify skill needs and implement nationwide, industry-led, collaborative skills development and entrepreneurship development initiatives for green jobs.

> India's energy future, as enunciated by Prime Minister Narendra Modi, has four pillars—energy access, energy efficiency, energy sustainability and energy security.

India is taking its experience of the renewable sector to the rest of the world by spearheading the International Solar Alliance (ISA). The ISA is an alliance of more than 121 sunshine countries that lie between the Tropics of Cancer and Capricorn. It was founded by India and France in 2015 to fight climate change and adopt solar energy by replacing fossil fuels. It aims to provide a dedicated platform for cooperation among these countries by assisting each other to achieve the common goals of increasing the use of solar energy in meeting energy needs, in a safe, convenient, affordable, equitable and sustainable manner. Prime Minister Modi, in the first assembly of the ISA, said that the ISA could replace OPEC as the key global energy supplier in the future.[14]

The world is attempting to fight climate change through a series of measures that can restrict the rise in temperate by 1.5 degrees. India's contribution and leadership in the RE sector will be critical to the success of these efforts.

---

[14]http://pib.nic.in/newsite/PrintRelease.aspx?relid=183908

9

THE ROLE OF SUSTAINABLE FINANCE IN SUPPORTING A GREEN ENERGY TRANSITION

Leveraging Private Finance to Achieve SDG 7 Targets and Beyond in India

Satya Sundar Tripathi

EXECUTIVE SUMMARY

It is widely recognized that public finance is insufficient for achieving the goals of improving equity, meeting climate change targets and ensuring affordable energy for all. Innovative sustainable finance approaches can play a critical role in unlocking capital from investors and private finance institutions, bringing monetary resources and capacity building into overlooked environmental sectors and fuelling transformational positive impacts. The effectiveness of blended finance's partnerships-based approach in leveraging private finance for public good is already evident in the agricultural sector in Indonesia, through the Tropical Landscapes Finance Facility's (TLFF) climate-smart and wildlife-friendly natural rubber project. Sustainable finance's demonstrated potential to result in triple-bottom-line benefits for livelihoods, natural capital and economic growth can then also be applicable in the energy sector to successfully provide a blueprint for meeting the objectives of Goal 7 of the Sustainable Development Goals (SDGs), and strengthen progress towards almost fifty-two of the 169 SDG targets. Till 2030, provide a critical opportunity for India to leverage private finance to deliver large-scale sustainability shifts in the energy sector and subsequently deliver cross-sectoral benefits that can create significant resilience to climate change impacts and better well-being for people at the same time.

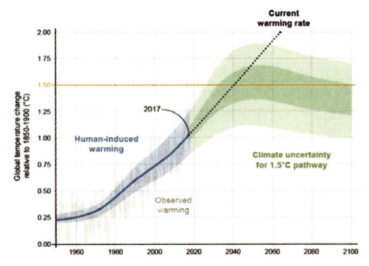

Figure 1: Global warming pathway. Human-induced warming reached approximately 1 ºC above pre-industrial levels in 2017.

Source: *See reference 1.*

GLOBAL CHALLENGE: CREATING RESILIENCE TO CLIMATE CHANGE IMPACTS

Human activities are responsible for causing 1 °C of global warming above pre-industrial levels (see Figure 1). Even if business-as-usual trends do not continue, it is likely that global warming will reach 1.5 °C between 2030 and 2052—as it continues to increase at the current rate,[1] leading to high risks for health, livelihoods, food security, water supply, human well-being and economic growth. While limiting warming to 1.5 °C is not impossible, the pace and scale of complex and necessary transitions across all sectors require a recognition that many governments lack the capacities, technical proficiency, regulations and financial resources required to deliver coordinated efforts at the levels needed to curb global warming at 1.5 °C. Thus, the 'well below 2.0 °C and aiming for 1.5 °C' scenario that the planet faces includes stress on water ecosystems in dry and tropical countries, greater frequency of storms, flooding, droughts and heat waves, worsening poverty and severe reduction in crop yields (see Figure 2).

Keeping this in mind, the next eleven years under the 2030 agenda provide a critical opportunity to utilize sustainable finance approaches to support countries in shifting to low emissions-based growth, and executing large-scale projects in regions that can deliver the greatest number of benefits in terms of livelihoods, climate, biodiversity, energy efficiency and access—while ensuring that there is progress in meeting the Paris Agreement and SDG targets. The role of innovative finance is particularly relevant, as the abatement costs of achieving the unconditional nationally determined contributions (NDCs) are estimated at $135 billion by 2030, while full implementation costs of the conditional NDCs are an additional $44–$55 billion.[2] Most developing countries lack these resources. The failure to build resilience at scale across sectors in the next eleven years would then have significant detrimental impacts across the world, as climate change impacts get worse.

KEY TO IMPACTS AND RISKS

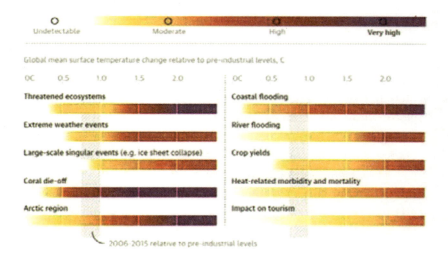

Figure 2: Projected impacts of temperature increases

Source: *http://report.ipcc.ch/sr15/pdf/sr15_spm_final.pdf (accessed on 15 January 2019)*

SIGNIFICANT POTENTIAL FOR ADVERSE SOCIAL, ENVIRONMENTAL AND ECONOMIC IMPACTS

Ninety per cent of coral reefs will be at the risk of elimination and there will be a 5 per cent decline in global fish biomass and fisheries production, per degree of warming.[3] It is estimated that climate-driven water scarcity could cost some regions up to 6 per cent of their GDP due to erratic water availability, leading to adverse impact on agriculture, incomes and health. Regions like Central Africa, East Asia and the Middle East are at higher risk, caused by rising demands of water with supply becoming increasingly uncertain.[4] Since 1.095 billion to 1.745 billion people depend on forests for their livelihoods, degradation of ecosystems and biodiversity will also have significant negative impacts on their climate resilience capacities.[5]

At a landscape level, agricultural systems are very vulnerable to climate change impacts, with increasing evidence that per degree of warming will result in an average reduction of 6 per cent in global wheat yields.[6] In Southern Africa, more than 30 per cent of maize could be lost by 2030 due to climate change.[7] In India, for example, any temperature increase would result in losses in wheat yields (see Figure 3). Agriculture provides livelihoods for 2.6 billion people and of the 525 million farms worldwide, approximately 404 million are less than two hectares. These small farms cultivate 60 per cent of arable land.[8] Unpredictable weather patterns will detrimentally affect the health of these farms and the ability of governments to meet the food security needs of almost nine billion people by 2050. Furthermore, the Bonn Challenge targets of restoring 350 million hectares by 2030 could be hindered unless scalable activities and projects are facilitated in priority regions of the world that can support the emergence of vetted climate resilient and deforestation-free commodity production strategies.

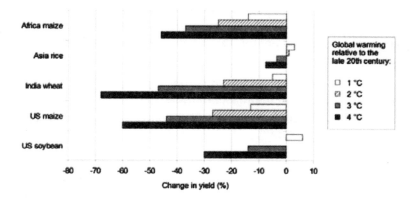

Figure 3: Effects on crop yields in countries

Source: *Figure 5.1, p. 161, in: Sec 5.1 Food production, prices, and hunger, in: Ch 5: 'Impacts in the Next Few Decades and Coming Centuries', in: US NRC 2011 (projections do not account for adaptation strategies)*

For the energy sector, changing precipitation patterns as temperatures increase will affect energy production and delivery. Supply of fossil fuels as well as thermal and hydropower generation and transmission will also be adversely impacted. As extreme weather events occur in greater numbers, there will be significant negative consequences for communities and economies rising from disasters causing widespread electricity outages and infrastructure losses. In 2012, for instance, twenty-five extreme weather events caused $188 billion in damages and 1,100 fatalities. Across the Northern Hemisphere, it is expected that global warming will reduce the availability of wind energy resources by 10 per cent to 40 per cent by 2050. The central US will be particularly affected, with declines ranging between 8–10 per cent by 2050—depending on whether a lower or higher greenhouse gases scenario is followed globally.[9] In regions such as southern Europe, southern US, southeast China and

South America, hydropower is projected to decrease by 5–20 per cent.[10] In terms of energy access, as distribution and affordability are impacted based on the capacities of developing countries to withstand climate change impacts, energy economics will need to consider critical social justice issues as well. Globally, 1.1 billion people lack access to affordable, reliable and clean energy.[11] Most of these households are in developing countries where traditional biomass is utilized for cooking and heating—which emits hazardous pollutants and chemicals that put women and children at the greatest risk. In India, for instance, 268,000 deaths in 2015 were directly caused by residential biomass fuel burning. The increased burden on local governments to mitigate climate change impacts while ensuring successful roll-out of, say, national biofuel policies is challenging due to resource constraints and technical capacities, which can lead to growing inequalities and worsening in condition of the poor—especially rural women and children.

MEETING GLOBAL GOALS BY 2030

The seventeen SDGs provide a common framework, with 169 targets that countries should aim to achieve by 2030. SDG 7 focuses on ensuring access to affordable, reliable and modern energy for all, while increasing the share of renewable energy in the global energy mix. India is in a strong position of operationalizing efforts towards meeting the SDGs. However, the 300 million unelectrified Indians pose a tremendous challenge in terms of delivering renewable, cost-effective and stable long-term access to energy. States and the private sector are expected to play a critical role in expanding infrastructure as well as in delivering profitable solutions, since the economic opportunity in energy access for India is estimated at $48 billion a year by 2030.

The Paris Agreement aims to keep the increase in global average temperature to well below 2 °C above pre-industrial levels, while limiting the increase to 1.5 °C to reduce risks associated with climate change and its effects. Scaling of renewable energy technology, with support from governments on large-scale deployment and implementation of policies, is required to meet the Paris Agreement targets. While renewable power generation is expected to grow more than 30 per cent between 2015 and 2020, the growth needs to be accelerated further by an additional 40 per cent between 2020 and 2025 to meet the 2 °C target.[12] More technological breakthroughs and new business models are required to fulfil this potential.[13]

> The economic opportunity in energy access for India is estimated at $48 billion a year by 2030.

The Bonn Challenge outlines a target of restoring 150 million hectares of the world's degraded and deforested lands by 2020 and 350 million hectares by 2030. Achieving this would result in a reduction of the current carbon emissions gap by 11–17 per cent and create $84 billion in benefits per year. Alternative sources of energy that are sustainable are required to reach these goals, with significant scaling through access to adequate fiscal resources. In Nigeria, for example, fuelwood collection is one of the greatest contributors to deforestation as almost 60 per cent of the rural population is dependent on it, with over 50 million metric tonnes of fuelwood consumed per year.[14] Shifting this dependence on traditional sources of energy can prevent further loss of natural capital and support Africa in meeting its commitment of restoring 55.3 million hectares—and for India, in reaching its 21 million hectare target. In India, this would deliver benefits equalling $6,594 million and 1.99 $GtCO_2$ sequestered by 2030.[15]

THE ROLE OF INNOVATIVE SUSTAINABLE FINANCE

There is a need to recognize the prevalent gaps in global financing and regional capacities, which can hamper the magnitude of impacts necessary to achieve the SDGs and other global targets within the limited time frame till 2030. It is widely recognized that public funding will not be enough to address the challenges the planet is facing. It is estimated that the global combined aid available for the development sector to address climate change impacts is around $150 billion, when what is required is close to $9 trillion. In terms of meeting SDG 7 targets on renewable energy, energy efficiency and universal energy access, the costs are expected to be between $1 billion and $1.3 billion per year until 2030.[16] It is only possible to meet these deficits with the involvement of the private sector and the large-scale financing it can generate through sustainable finance models.

Financial models that generate large-scale financing to address the complex challenges of engaging within and on behalf of 'nature', and adequate, sustainable economic, social and environmental returns, are required. Such models can create winning financial environments within which countries can progress towards meeting their energy transition goals. Innovative sustainable finance enables access to fiscal resources with lower interest rates, longer payback periods and distributed risk models. They empower projects in often financially overlooked sectors like forestry, fisheries, renewable energy, wildlife conservation, deforestation-free commodity production and so on, to emerge with competitive business models that also promote equity, economic competitiveness and achievement of global goals like SDG 7.

Instead of a conventional 'concentrated risk' approach where all the risk is concentrated in the hands of the borrower, the blended finance approach mainstreams a unique 'distributed' risk model that has a host of significant actors assuming bits of the risk along the value chain, making the projects 'investable'. This enables the provision of financing to sectors that typically do not qualify for loans due to an inability to provide returns within short repayment periods and with high interest rates. The combination of credit guarantees ensure that capital can be made available at rates notably below current market rates for a duration that allows the projects to generate returns—while ensuring considerable social, environmental and financial returns.

ACHIEVING TRIPLE-BOTTOM-LINE BENEFITS IN COUNTRIES

In many countries, sustainable finance models are already engendering a blended finance revolution by unlocking capital from investors and private finance institutions. They are bringing monetary resources and capacity building to effectively support countries in transitioning to the greening of sectors like forestry, agriculture, etc., and resulting in transformational positive impacts on the ground. In Indonesia, a multi-stakeholder group consisting of UN Environment, World Agroforestry Center, BNP Paribas and ADM Capital established the TLFF, which was launched in October 2016. This innovative platform, the world's first, is helping Indonesia work towards its strategic development goals and its climate change targets. In doing so, Indonesia has become the leading country in the world to pioneer a facility that leverages public funding to unlock private finance in both renewable energy production and sustainable land use, including in agriculture and restoration. The TLFF aims to lend $1 billion by 2019 and on 26 February 2018, announced its inaugural transaction—a landmark $95 million sustainability bond to help finance a $350 million sustainable natural rubber plantation on heavily degraded land in two provinces in Indonesia. It will generate employment for 16,000 people and make 50,000 people living in remote areas more resilient to climate change impacts. The bond is the first corporate sustainable bond in Asia and the first sustainability bond in the Association of South East Asian Nations (ASEAN). The TLFF is a model that is applicable and scalable in other emerging economies to unlock capital from institutional investors and other private finance institutions for achieving green development and climate resilience goals.

There is potential to deliver considerable cross-sectoral impacts and new economic opportunities in Indonesia through innovative finance, with additional projects doing everything from financing the activities of smallholders in coconut sugar, palm oil and cocoa to improving dairy, fisheries and land rehabilitation practices. Each of these projects would deliver triple-bottom-line impacts by generating local economic revenues, green jobs and better management of ecosystems and biodiversity. They will also provide Indonesia's provincial governments with models for effective green development planning.

In India, through sustainable finance approaches led by the Sustainable India Finance Facility, investments equalling $2.3 billion will transform the work of six million farmers and 8 million hectares to 100 per cent chemical-free and natural agriculture by 2024.

The government of Andhra Pradesh is leading an unprecedented transformation towards sustainable agriculture at a massive scale that will make the state India's first zero budget natural farming (ZBNF) state, while enhancing resilience of smallholders in varying agro-climatic zones, promoting gender-sensitive development and providing an opportunity to reclaim planetary boundaries. The overall benefits of ZBNF include: (a) provision of low cost bio-organic fertilizers, (b) consistent yields, (c) restoration of ecosystem services, (d) preservation of habitats for biodiversity, (e) use of local seeds, (f) multi-cropping with tree cover, (g) ability of farms to withstand extreme climatic events, (h) safe and nutritious food, (i) improvements in health for farmers as well as consumers and (j) empowerment of women farmers. As of November 2018, 500,000 farmers and 495,000 hectares have been converted to chemical-free farming.[17] At completion, this system-scale transformation will provide a best-practice example of ecologically conscious and smallholder-friendly food production. It will also give governments a replicable strategy to deliver a widespread shift away from conventional food production and management of the agriculture sector.

STRENGTHENING PROGRESS TOWARDS SDG 7 TARGETS IN INDIA

Background of the energy sector in India

India has a background of strong and active engagement by the government in the energy sector in terms of providing 'hard' and 'soft' policy measures, with the provision of cost-effective energy supply and improving connectivity being the key areas of focus. In 2015, the International Solar Alliance was launched by Prime Minister Narendra Modi, making India a leader in terms of promoting collaboration with neighbouring countries on knowledge exchange and technology transfer. The Pradhan Mantri Ujjwala Yojana scheme was launched by the government in May 2016 to enable poor and rural households across the country to shift to the use of cleaner cooking fuels. In this scheme, there is a particular focus on forest dwellers, most backward classes, tea and ex-tea garden tribes and people residing in islands to ensure that marginalized households are provided with low-cost and efficient alternatives such as liquefied petroleum gas (LPG) connections to improve their overall well-being. The main objectives of the scheme are to (a) empower women and improve their well-being, (b) reduce the negative impacts on health caused by cooking with sources like coal, fuelwood, etc., (c) reduce number of deaths from unclean cooking fuels and (d) protect young children from respiratory illnesses related to indoor pollution caused by burning of fossil fuels.

Additionally, India's biofuel policy was announced in May 2018, aiming to reduce the country's emissions and energy imports while expanding the scope of 'biofuel' feedstock to include industrial waste along with agricultural sources.[19] The policy seeks to mobilize greater action from public and private actors, as biofuel production in India is much lower than its potential. In terms of overall performance on SDG 7, since 2012, there has been consistent growth in installed electricity generation capacity with 51.3 per cent growth in the installed capacity of non-fossil-fuel sectors. The installed capacity of the renewable energy (wind, solar, bio and small- hydro power) sector has also more than doubled.[20] Out of the 1.2 billion people who have gained energy access globally since 2000, 500 million live in India.[21] Furthermore, investments in clean energy in India rose 22 per cent in the first half of 2018, compared to the same period the previous year. Since 2014, $42 billion has been invested in renewable energy, which will generate business opportunities equalling $70 billion–$80 billion in the green energy space over four years. By the late 2020s, India is expected to become the largest growth market in clean energy, overtaking China.

Existing challenges

While there is considerable progress in shifting to clean energy in India, significant challenges still exist in terms of adequate accounting of social and environmental externalities along with a continuing need to adopt an integrated SDGs-focused approach that is supported by sufficient amount of funding. It is estimated that 100 million households still rely on fuelwood, coal, cow dung cakes and so on for their primary cooking needs in the country. This has significant impacts on health, as hazardous air pollutants (HAP) emitted during the burning of such biomass are linked with low birth weight in children, acute respiratory infections in children below the age of 5 and pulmonary diseases as well as lung cancer in women. In 2015, approximately 977,094 deaths in India were associated with exposure to household air pollution (HAP), with a significant number of women and children among those affected.[22] More specifically, a study by IIT Bombay and the Health Effects Institute found that 268,000 deaths in 2015 were directly caused by residential biomass fuel burning. An analysis by the Council on Energy, Environment and Water across six states—Uttar Pradesh, Bihar, Jharkhand, Odisha, West Bengal and Madhya Pradesh—revealed that 8.4 per cent of households under the Tier 0 category (lowest access to energy) also face challenges of insufficient food due to limited availability of cooking fuels.[23] This has vital implications for access to nutrition for large segments of India's population.

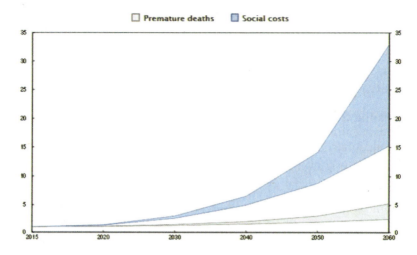

Figure 4: Trends in India caused by outdoor air pollution

Source: *https://oecdinsights.org/2017/11/14/urgent-action-on-air-pollution-in-india-makes-economic-sense/*

In addition to health consequences, the lack of access to clean cooking fuels contributes to increasing inequity and widening social disparity, which can impede the ability of India to meet its development and climate targets. Nearly 40 per cent of India's air pollution comes from household fuel burning. Research has found linkages between black carbon emissions and greater solar absorption, which contributes to the melting of Himalayan glaciers and can cause surface dimming, lowering crop productivity.[24] An examination by Singh et al (2017) also shows that non-renewable biomass promotes deforestation and forest degradation due to significant extractive fuelwood collection. It was estimated that increasing adoption of LPG in India from 2001 to 2011 led to a net emission reduction of 6.73 $MtCO_2e$ based on avoided fuelwood displaced.[25] Moreover, at least thirteen out of the seventeen SDGs[26] are directly or indirectly related to equal energy access, food security and creation of resilient societies, making clean fuels critical for India's progress towards achieving the SDGs.

In addition, most efforts thus far have targeted energy efficiency gains without taking into account climate gains appropriately. India's emissions trajectory is largely driven by income growth due to high rates of urbanization and increasing levels of economic growth. This trajectory is mainly influenced by the energy intensity of GDP instead of carbon intensity drivers. The national policy framework has identified the need to focus on low carbon growth, but the share of renewable energy as a part of total energy supply still has significant scope for further growth.[27] Several challenges exist for the energy sector and its green transition to successfully meet SDG 7 targets, a number of which can be addressed through innovative sustainable finance and its partnerships-based approach that overcomes public sector funding barriers and delivers more widespread contribution from the private sector. These challenges include:[28]

- Creation and improvement of off-grid transmission infrastructure that brings connectivity into remote areas through decentralized renewable energy projects, fostered by sustainable business models generated through entrepreneurship in renewable energy.
- Rapid scaling up of existing off-grid programmes that are supported by the necessary policy-related changes and incentives.
- Mitigation of negative social and environmental externalities such as dam construction, flooding, deforestation, displacement of communities, to name a few that are associated

with hydro, wind and nuclear energy.
- Determining what policy changes will be required based on the growing energy consumption and demand profiles of cities that will increasingly exert greater influence on energy transition trends.
- Widespread application of profitable renewable energy ventures that have scope for large-scale financing.
- Addressing air quality deterioration and prevention of inequitable impacts on women and children in rural areas.

Finally, while India has committed to renewable energy being 40 per cent of the country's projected electricity capacity by 2030, the scaling up and investment required to achieve this target is estimated at $189 billion by 2022. However, it is likely that investments could fall short by 29 per cent ($17 billion) for equity and 27 per cent ($36 billion) for debt.[29] Thus, the role of less conventional financial instruments is critical and this is only possible through private sector investments.

SUPPORTING A GREEN ENERGY TRANSITION THROUGH INNOVATIVE SUSTAINABLE FINANCE IN INDIA

Innovative sustainable finance has the potential to deliver transformational impacts by catalysing collaborations at the appropriate levels in order to mobilize investments in renewable energy projects that would otherwise not be available through traditional resource flows. The potential of innovative sustainable finance approaches—to deliver buy-in from stakeholders and engage the private sector at the scale necessary in agricultural commodity production—is already demonstrated through the TLFF's inaugural $350 million project, which then presents a significant opportunity for the energy sector. On 12 December 2017, UN Environment and BNP Paribas signed a memorandum of understanding with a target capital funding amount of $10 billion by 2025, aiming to identify suitable commercial projects in smallholder agriculture, energy access, agroforestry, fisheries, air quality and biodiversity—among other sectors—in developing countries where there are large measurable environment and social impacts possible. There is, therefore, financing available in addition to the opportunities for capacity strengthening through partnerships, which can be availed for a successful transition of the energy sector in India and also result in large-scale cross-sectoral benefits for health, poverty, gender, ecosystems and climate resilience. Specifically, the following impacts could be achieved through blended finance:

Meeting the targets for SDGs 3, 5, 6, 8 and 13: An integrated and SDGs-focused strategy could be adopted as a key part of 'last-mile' electricity access efforts, to result in better poverty alleviation and sustainable development. For example, studies have shown improvements in delivery of health services through the treatment of 50 per cent more outpatients each month with the introduction of rooftop solar infrastructure in villages in India. Blended finance could support the aggregation of such projects that have revenue generation potential and provide much-needed funding and partnership support to roll out large-scale, low-cost infrastructure, so that the SDG 3 targets of good health and well-being are achieved locally. Furthermore, women entrepreneurs, through companies like Frontier Markets, have demonstrated profitability as sales agents for solar products by providing access to electric rice hullers that resulted in a hundredfold increase in outputs and a $400 additional income on average. As shareholders are interested in gender-specific impacts, women-based sustainable business ideas could be scaled through blended finance models, achieving greater gender equality (SDG 5). Clean water targets under SDG 6 can be supported through funding for widespread application of innovative solutions that bring together reverse osmosis filtering technology with mini-grids to provide affordable drinking water. Additionally, villages connected to mini-grids have shown an $18.50 per capita increase in GDP+ (which measures economic GDP and a valuation of social and environmental benefits), supporting progress towards SDG 8 by strengthening economic growth and generating decent work opportunities. The flexibility in structuring—to reduce risk under sustainable finance approaches—can enhance the ability of entrepreneurs to procure funding for such green ventures compared to hindrances faced under public financing mechanisms. Decentralized energy infrastructure can contribute to creating resilience to climate change and is thus a valuable adaptation strategy for climate action (SDG 13). Renewable energy-based mini-grids played a significant role in recovery during the August 2017 floods in the state of Bihar, by supplying backup power when existing infrastructure was damaged.[30] Evidence exists across various parts of India of effective sustainability solutions in the energy sector, which could be considerably scaled through blended finance—delivering progress beyond SDG 7 to meet at least fifty-two of the 169 targets of the SDGs.

> India has committed to renewable energy being 40 per cent of the country's projected electricity capacity by 2030.

Strengthening state government capacities: Several state governments in India have a number of effective policies and incentives promoting energy efficiency and renewable energy. The solar rooftop programme in Odisha is an example of the recognition of the role that access to affordable energy plays in the education and health of individuals. As grid-connected rooftop solar systems are increasingly adopted by households in Odisha, it would be valuable to assess where need gaps exist, to enable successful replication of these programmes in other states—which innovative sustainable finance can support by bridging gaps. Moreover, while policies in India seek to mobilize greater action by public and private actors, renewable energy production in biofuel, etc. is much lower than its potential. Sustainable finance and partnerships-based structuring support for setting up supply chains, ethanol plants and procurement mechanisms can increase the utilization of agricultural waste from 170 million tonnes to 250 million tonnes per year resulting in production of 31–47 billion litres of ethanol by 2020, compared to the 2 billion litres currently produced. The improved efficiency and quantity of crop residues utilized could benefit the health of 7 per cent of the world's population, which resides in northern India and is adversely affected by crop residue burning every winter—resulting in extreme deterioration of air quality. Such scale would be challenging to achieve for state governments without innovative sustainable finance-based collaborations.

Opportunity for decent green jobs: Furthermore, by 2025, India's demographic dividend will create the need for significant employment opportunities that could be met by greening of the energy sector. It is estimated that more than 300,000 jobs could be provided if India meets its targets of 100 GW of solar and 60 GW of wind energy capacities by 2022. But budgetary deficits persisting that hinder the achievement of most of these targets by 2030. Innovative blended finance models (debt, grant, public, private)—structured around payment for performance and shared accountability mechanisms, multi-stakeholder collaboration and delivery—could be incentivized improving the chances of these efforts to garner the support needed for creating more fair wage jobs, compared to business-as-usual scenarios under conventional sources of financing.

> It is estimated that more than 300,000 jobs could be provided if India meets its targets of 100 GW of solar and 60 GW of wind energy capacities by 2022.

REFERENCES

1. IPCC, 2018: Summary for Policymakers. In: Global warming of 1.5°C. An IPCC Special Report on the impacts of global warming of 1.5°C above pre-industrial levels and related global greenhouse gas emission pathways, in the context of strengthening the global response to the threat of climate change, sustainable development, and efforts to eradicate poverty [V. Masson-Delmotte, P. Zhai, H. O. Pörtner, D. Roberts, J. Skea, P. R. Shukla, A. Pirani, W. Moufouma-Okia, C. Péan, R. Pidcock, S. Connors, J. B. R. Matthews, Y. Chen, X. Zhou, M. I. Gomis, E. Lonnoy, T. Maycock, M. Tignor, T. Waterfield (eds)]. World Meteorological Organization, Geneva, Switzerland, 32 pp. http://report.ipcc.ch/sr15/pdf/sr15_spm_final.pdf
2. Andries F.Hof et al. (2017) 'Global and regional abatement costs

of Nationally Determined Contributions (NDCs) and of enhanced action to levels well below 2 °C and 1.5 °C', *Environmental Science & Policy* 71: 30–40. https://www.sciencedirect.com/science/article/pii/S1462901116308978

3. Simon Dietz et al. (2018) 'The Economics of 1.5–C Climate Change', *Annu. Rev. Environ. Resour.* 43:455–480. https://www.annualreviews.org/doi/pdf/10.1146/annurev-environ-102017-025817

4. World Bank. 2016. 'High and Dry: Climate Change, Water, and the Economy.' Executive Summary. World Bank, Washington, DC. http://www.worldbank.org/en/topic/water/publication/high-and-dry-climate-change-water-and-the-economy

5. D.K. Langat et al. (2016) 'Role of Forest Resources to Local Livelihoods: The Case of East Mau Forest Ecosystem, Kenya', *International Journal of Forestry Research*. https://www.hindawi.com/journals/ijfr/2016/4537354/

6. Roz Pidcock (2016) Scientists compare climate change impacts at 1.5C and 2C, Carbon Brief. https://www.carbonbrief.org/scientists-compare-climate-change-impacts-at-1-5c-and-2c

7. Lobell DB, Burke MB, Tebaldi C, Mastrandrea MD, Falcon WP, Naylor RL (2008). "Prioritizing climate change adaptation needs for food security in 2030". Science. 319 (5863): 607–10.

8. UNEP – Green Economy Initiative

9. Kristopher B. Karnauskas et al. (2018) 'Southward shift of the global wind energy resource under high carbon dioxide emissions', *Nature Geoscience* 11: 38–43. https://www.nature.com/articles/s41561-017-0029-9.epdf?referrer_access_token=LJamNUyn_zIcXphQab7FdRgN0jAjWe l9jnR3ZoTv0P49rtWtL3NDfrMbC8 PsMj ZGgZqF_9gec8nvisRPw4zeo4Ch Mi20ui X4xVjnEq5kEX3ChibVR Xczoc7AmdtAmSeZvBUNQAN5ZeXzATCPDbe9p1_iZI8j DH0Gj2V4mXaCspmpD2ScF6JiyZytQae9qWUriTxDhUUkLQ_aU8exsQtCIYa2WYWiU BU60q AymWMu49uxTP6KIuz EP X1V vNT4BgtE7jiahKxPhJMo0Ybw kGRAZqqtz M1Ntqojc4gky8fvrOcNPBKr dd1om WQt4 KQ7TReY1b BRsI4AaOl9Abj2siGUna dXTJkjYKxG cQOaps SnUD SPLE PAmuDatm2E6nOZUO 6CYyemDtsjhNy3QOCQjA%3D%3D&tr

177

acking_referrer=www.washingtonpost.com
10. Jennifer Cronin et al. (2018) 'Climate change impacts on the energy system: a review of trends and gaps,' *Climate Change* 151(2): 79 – 93. https://link.springer.com/article/10.1007/s10584-018-2265-4
11. World Resources Institute n.d. https://www.wri.org/our-work/project/energy-access
12. UNFCCC, 2017. https://unfccc.int/news/world-energy-system-not-on-track-to-meet-paris-agreement-goals
13. UNFCCC, 2017. https://unfccc.int/news/clean-energy-can-meet-90-of-paris-energy-related-goals
14. Nuraddeen A. Maiwada et al. (2014) 'The Role of Renewable Energy in Mitigating Deforestation and Climate Change in Nigeria', *Journal of Natural Sciences Research* 4(24): 81 – 84. http://citeseerx.ist.psu.edu/viewdoc/download?doi=10.1.1.662.4468&rep=rep1&type=pdf
15. http://www.bonnchallenge.org/content/india
16. UNDP and UN Environment (2018) Financing SDG 7, Policy Brief #5 https://sustainabledevelopment.un.org/content/documents/17549PB_5_Draft.pdf
17. Saurabh Tripathi et al. (2018) Zero Budget Natural Farming for the Sustainable Development Goals, Andhra Pradesh, India. Council on Energy, Environment and Water, Delhi. http://apzbnf.in/wp-content/uploads/2018/11/CEEW-ZBNF-Issue-Brief-2nd-Edition-PRINT-READY-20Sep18-min.pdf
18. Cabinet Committee on Economic Affairs, Press Release (2018). http://pib.nic.in/newsite/PrintRelease.aspx?relid=176351
19. India Country Commercial Guide, 2018. https://www.export.gov/apex/article2?id=India-Energy
20. India: Voluntary National Review on the Implementation of the Sustainable Development Goals, 2017. http://niti.gov.in/writereaddata/files/India%20VNR_Final.pdf
21. IISD, 2017. http://sdg.iisd.org/commentary/guest-articles/india-interlinking-the-sdgs-through-electricity-access/
22. Public Health Foundation of India and Center for Environmental Health (2017) https://www.ceh.org.in/wp-content/uploads/2017/10/Air-Pollution-and-Health-in-India.pdf

23. Council on Energy, Environment and Water, Columbia University and Practical Action (2017) http://ceew.in/pdf/CEEW%20-%20Measuring%20Energy%20Access%20in%20India%20Practical%20Action%20Briefing%20Paper%20Feb17.pdf
24. Rehman, *et al* (2011) in *Atmospheric Chemistry and Physics*. http://www-ramanathan.ucsd.edu/files/pr178.pdf
25. Singh, *et al* (2017) in *Environmental Research Letters*. http://iopscience.iop.org/article/10.1088/1748-9326/aa909d/pdf
26. See indicators under SDGs 1, 2, 3, 5, 7, 8, 9, 10, 11, 12, 13, 15 and 17. https://sustainabledevelopment.un.org/sdgs
27. Kenrick Mascarenhas et al. (2017) *Affordable and Clean Energy: An Indian Perspective*. Indian Institute for Human Settlements. http://iihs.co.in/knowledge-gateway/wp-content/uploads/2017/10/Affordable-and-Clean-Energy-An-Indian-Perspective.pdf
28. *Ibid*
29. Gireesh Shrimali (2018) *Renewable Energy: Solutions to the Financing Challenge*. Center for Asian Studies. https://www.ifri.org/sites/default/files/atoms/files/shrimali_renewable_energy_india_2018.pdf
30. IISD, 2017. http://sdg.iisd.org/commentary/guest-articles/india-interlinking-the-sdgs-through-electricity-access/

10

A NEW PARADIGM IN ENERGY DIPLOMACY

S. Jaishankar

A noteworthy feature of Indian diplomacy under the current government is the degree to which it is now closely linked to national development goals. Foreign policy outcomes increasingly highlight international partnerships that directly contribute to economic growth and modernization, including through capacity building and best practices. The themes of our national campaigns in fields as diverse as digital development, skills, smart cities and start-ups feature prominently in the contemporary diplomatic agenda. The most visible example of this shift in paradigm relates to the field of energy. It has become a significant vehicle to promote cooperation in our neighbourhood, one that aims at strengthening regional self-reliance. Ensuring greater energy security has been another objective that has been made possible by forging bonds of friendship in our extended neighbourhood and beyond. The diversification of energy sources has widened choices and produced more competitive options. The priority assigned to energy diplomacy is evident in India's higher profile in international forums and mechanisms dealing with the subject.

S. JAISHANKAR ▸

INDIA'S HYDROCARBON DIPLOMACY IN SOUTH ASIA AND THE INDIAN OCEAN REGION

Figure 1

The 'neighbourhood first' policy of the government is designed to underline the greater importance attached to relationships in South Asia. This was visible from the very inauguration of the government, at which the leaders of our neighbours were all present. The approach is predicated on the belief that India's prosperity is a larger lifting tide for the entire region. Unfortunately, the politics of South Asia till recently discouraged the development of connectivity and shared developmental endeavours. That has started to change and the more positive sentiment is being harnessed to accelerate greater economic cooperation. Naturally, addressing growing energy demands is of great significance as it directly impacts both growth prospects and quality of life. India can make the difference to the entire region not just due to its geographical centrality, but also because it can bring to bear scale and capacities in a manner that would benefit its neighbours. In India itself, higher incomes and more inclusive growth has steadily pushed up energy consumption. The same story is happening in different ways across the whole regional geography. Energy, once a source of divisiveness, today holds the potential of driving the regional integration process.

India's neighbours see it as a reliable energy partner who is helping them in building their own energy security and infrastructure. Nepal is among India's oldest regional partners in this sector and has been sourcing all its petroleum product requirements since the 1970s. The contract between Indian Oil and Nepal Oil Corporation was renewed for another five years in March 2017. To make supplies more weather-proof, efficient and cost-effective, the two countries have embarked on a 69 km petroleum product pipeline from Motihari in India to Amlekhgunj in Nepal. Its groundbreaking ceremony was held in April 2018. Since then, over 70 per cent of the pipeline has already been completed. The Nepalese side, seeing advantages of pipeline connectivity, has requested extension of the pipeline to Chitwan, as well as similar pipelines for liquefied petroleum gas (LPG) and natural gas. Indian companies have also played a key role in the setting up of a petroleum skill development centre in Janakpur in Nepal. Cooperation in the energy sector underlines India's role as an indispensable partner for Nepal's development.

With Bangladesh, India is constructing a 130-km pipeline between Siliguri in India and Parbatipur, which will supply 1 million metric tonnes of diesel to the Bangladesh Petroleum Corporation (BPC) for twenty years. The Indo-Bangla Friendship Pipeline, for which Prime Minister Narendra Modi and Prime Minister Sheikh Hasina witnessed the groundbreaking in September 2018, is being constructed under a grant from the Government of India. Till the pipeline becomes operational, Numaligarh Refinery is supplying diesel by rail rakes. Indian companies are also working on building a land-based liquefied natural gas (LNG) terminal to augment supply of natural gas to Bangladesh, as well as a pipeline to the Jessore-Khulna power plant across the Panitar and Satkhira border points on the Indian and Bangladeshi sides respectively. The pipeline will supply regasified LNG from the upcoming Dhamra LNG terminal in Odisha. As a matter of goodwill, India supplied 20,000 cooking stoves and kerosene oil to refugees in the Cox's Bazar area. Bangladesh, on its part, is supplying LPG from its storage facilities in Chittagong to demand centres in Tripura. This relationship has thus demonstrated how political goodwill can overcome handicaps of geography.

> The priority assigned to energy diplomacy is evident in India's higher profile in international forums and mechanisms dealing with the subject.

Sri Lanka has seen the presence of Indian Oil in the retail sector for the last fifteen years, which has led to the modernization of the sector. India is now creating LNG infrastructure in Sri Lanka—the first of its kind—in partnership with a Japanese company, to help the country move to cleaner sources of power generation and, eventually, transportation and domestic cooking fuel. India's presence in the Trincomalee tank farms could boost the island nation's energy security and the future creation of a petroleum hub.

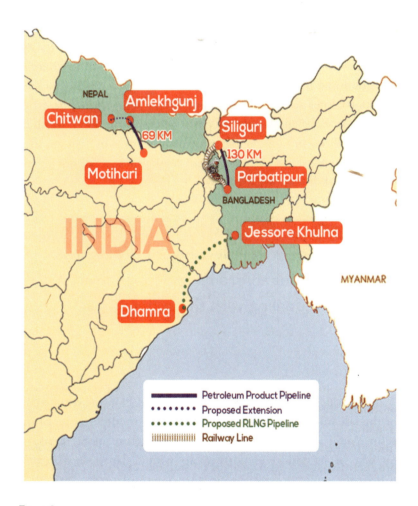

Figure 2

India also continues to be a reliable supplier of 100 per cent of petroleum product requirements of Mauritius through Mangalore Refinery and Petrochemical Limited (MRPL) since 2006. Indian Oil has been present in the energy sector of Mauritius since 2004 covering retail, bunkering, lubricants and consumer sales. It is the leading supplier of jet fuel in Mauritius. In order to harness the strategic location of Mauritius as a base for bunkering the exports to countries of East and South East Africa, a detailed project report (DPR) is being prepared to set up petroleum storage and bunkering facilities in Albion.

India's plans to develop infrastructure in Myanmar also include an oil and gas complement. Indian Oil is engaged in doing a feasibility study for building a refinery at Thanlyin, close to Yangon. A proposal is also under consideration to set up an LNG terminal to augment gas supply as feedstock for the country's growing electricity requirement. To reduce logistics costs in ferrying petroleum products from Yangon to the north-eastern parts of Myanmar, close to Indian borders, Numaligarh Refinery is supplying diesel by land route across the Moreh–Tamu border. To expand the supplies of petroleum products and maintain a buffer, a storage facility is being considered close to Tamu on the Myanmar side.

India continues to supply 100 per cent of the petroleum products requirement of Bhutan. The Bhutanese Government is planning to extend 100 per cent LPG coverage by end 2018 from its current penetration of nearly 38 per cent. This additional product demand is envisaged to be supplied from the refineries in Assam. India is also working with the Bhutanese Government to share the experience of the successfully implemented PMUY, for implementation in Bhutan.

> In India itself, higher incomes and more inclusive growth have steadily pushed up energy consumption.

INDIA-UAE strategic partnership

Abu Dhabi National Oil Company invested $400 MN in Strategic Petroleum Reserve (SPR) storage facility in Mangalore ensuring energy security in India.

1st Foreign investment in India's SPR

Total Capacity **5.86 MN** Barrels

Crude Storage Saving **₹3500 Cr** for India

ADNOC signed an MoU in November 2018 to consider filling another two caverns in Padur, Karnataka.

Indian acquisition in UAE

In February 2018, a consortium of Indian companies acquired **10% stake** in **Lower Zakhum** offshore oil fields of UAE.

Figure 3

Keeping pace with the expanding comprehensive strategic partnerships with the countries in India's extended neighbourhood, such as the UAE and Saudi Arabia, some major landmarks have been achieved in the oil and gas sector. In 2018 ADNOC, the national oil company of the UAE, became the first overseas company to fill approximately 5.9 million barrels of its crude oil in the strategic petroleum reserve (SPR) cavern in Mangaluru. An MoU was signed in November 2018 in Abu Dhabi for ADNOC to consider filling another two caverns in Padur, Karnataka. The UAE has also been India's first destination for upstream investment in the high-prestige Gulf region. In February 2018, a consortium of Indian companies invested over $600 million in acquiring a 10 per cent stake in the prolific Lower Zakhum offshore oilfields. This transformed the decades old buyer–seller relationship to one of strategic two-way investments. In April 2018, Indian Oil also acquired a 17 per cent stake in the Mukhaizna Oilfield in Oman. New openings have also been made with Saudi Arabia in April 2018. Saudi Aramco signed an MoU to become a 50 per cent partner in the 60 mmt Ratnagiri greenfield refinery, the largest planned greenfield refinery in the world, with an investment of about US $44 billion. Aramco has further partnered with ADNOC in this major energy initiative.

Figure 4

OVERSEAS ACQUISITIONS IN THE LAST FOUR YEARS

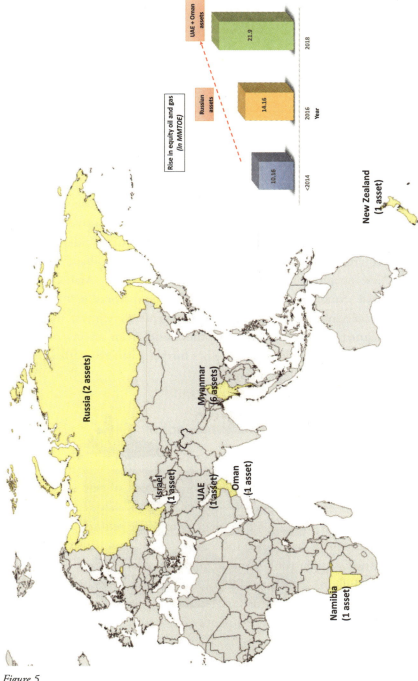

Figure 5

Figure 6

The last few years have also witnessed a new approach for overseas assets acquisition. Preference has been given to investing in producing fields which provide immediate returns. It is no mean achievement that today, Indian oil and gas companies are present in twenty-eight countries with investments worth approximately US $38 billion. The share of equity oil and gas for the year 2017–18 for Indian public sector undertakings (PSUs) from these assets was around 22 million metric tonnes of oil equivalent (mmtoe) per year.

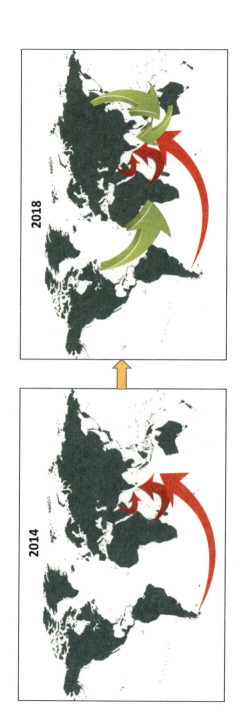

Figure 7

With two-way investments of a strategic nature between India and Russia, a veritable energy bridge has been built. Four public sector oil companies together acquired a 49.9 per cent stake in Vankorneft, the second largest producing field of Russia, and a 29.9 per cent one in Tass Yurakh at a total investment of over US $5.5 billion. This has made Russia the largest overseas investment destination in the oil and gas sector. Russia also became the largest overseas investor in India's oil and gas sector by investing about $13 billion in acquiring the Vadinar Refinery of Essar (now NAYARA Energy).

> It is no mean achievement that today, Indian oil and gas companies are present in twenty-eight countries with investments worth approximately US $38 billion.

In an effort to reduce overreliance on a few geographies for crude supplies, India has further diversified crude sourcing by importing crude from non-traditional sources such as the US since October 2017. This was also a follow-up to a Strategic Energy Partnership announced by Prime Minister Modi and President Trump in July 2017 in Washington, DC. Between 2017–18, more than twenty-five million barrels of US crude have been imported by Indian public sector refiners, thereby reducing the trade deficit by $2 billion. India also received the first consignment of US LNG in March 2018 under a twenty-year GAIL contract. This alone will contribute over $2 billion to bilateral trade and further offset the trade imbalance. Import of crude from the US is likely to go up much further in 2019 once port and pipeline infrastructure in the US gets completed. India has also leveraged its large and growing market for natural gas to renegotiate its long-term LNG supply deals with Qatar, Australia and Russia to the advantage of its consumers.

The last few years have also witnessed increasing engagement on the part of India with international oil and gas organizations. India chaired the International Energy Forum (IEF) over 2016–18, which comprises countries contributing at least 90 per cent to global energy consumption and production. The leadership of this organization culminated in India's hosting the sixteenth edition of the IEF ministerial meetings in New Delhi in 2018, which saw the participation of about forty ministers, ten heads of international organizations and about thirty CEOs. India also initiated an institutional dialogue with the Organization of Petroleum Exporting Countries (OPEC) in December 2015 and has maintained regular meetings between the Secretary General, OPEC, and India's Minister of Petroleum and Natural Gas. India also became an association country in the Paris-based International Energy Agency (IEA) in March 2017. It is a testimony to the importance attached to expanding energy cooperation and ensuring energy security that global captains of the oil and gas sector meet regularly with the key leadership of the Indian Government.

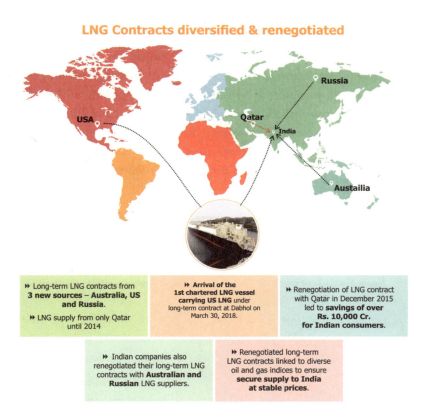

Figure 8

International fora such as OPEC and the IEF have provided India a platform which has been used effectively to convey issues of interest and concern to India, such as giving the call for reasonable and responsible pricing that serves the interests of both producers and consumers, as well as elimination of Asian premium and the inflexibilities and obesity of the LNG trading architecture.

The leadership demonstrated in promoting India's international engagement in the oil and gas sector has ensured that there is greater appreciation of its concerns and interests. It is significant that major Gulf exporters are more open-minded on the Asian Premium than in the past. Already, the Premium announced for January 2019 has gone down considerably from previous months, resulting in a potential saving of over $75 million for the month of January 2019 for import of crude from Saudi Arab, Kuwait and Iraq. India's active participation in global energy discussions is evoking a positive response—and there is an expectation that its concerns would be taken into account by major oil producers when they make key decisions.

DECLINE IN ASIAN PREMIUM

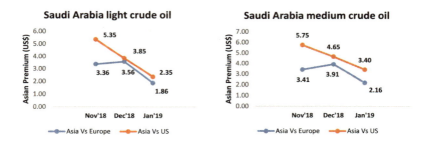

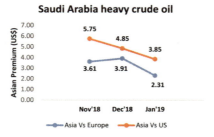

Figure 9

All in all, recent initiatives have contributed to a higher Indian profile in the energy sector as a consumer, supplier and investor. Our responsible policies have not only strengthened stability in the energy markets but also provided a large segment of South Asian societies more affordable access to power and energy. The shifting paradigm in the energy sector is truly a case of diplomacy for development.

11

INDIA: THE DUAL CHALLENGE AND ENERGY INVESTMENT OPPORTUNITIES

Bob Dudley

INTRODUCTION

The global energy industry faces the dual challenge of meeting society's need for more energy, while producing and delivering it in new ways with fewer greenhouse gas emissions. The energy sector is changing faster than at any other time in our lifetime with the energy mix shifting towards lower carbon sources, driven by technological advances and growing environmental concerns. This is a time of transformational change.

India is at the forefront of these changes. In the past thirty years, the global population has risen by two billion to a total of more than seven billion, with India set to become the world's most populous nation within the next few years. Life expectancy has risen globally by an average of seven years in that time, and by ten years in India. Meanwhile, global GDP has more than tripled—from under $20 trillion to well over $70 trillion—with India's GDP increasing faster still, going up nearly tenfold.

This progress has been supported by huge growth in global energy, as hundreds of millions of people in emerging economies, like India's, have been lifted out of low incomes. India is predicted to overtake China as the largest growth market for energy by the late 2020s.

Our challenge as a sector is to produce energy and help meet the challenge of the world's climate goals as they were set out in Paris in 2015—to limit the global temperature rise to well below 2°C, compared to pre-industrial times—as well as help address environmental concerns such as urban air quality. This requires a diversity of resources, managed in a coordinated way, where renewables and nuclear are utilised along with hydrocarbons.

INDIA AND THE DUAL CHALLENGE

As one of the world's largest and fastest-growing economies, what happens in India has a real impact on both elements of the dual challenge—meeting demand and reducing emissions.

India is working hard to spread the benefits of a growing economy among its population of more than 1.3 billion—around 30 per cent of whom do not currently have access to modern sources of energy.

This economic growth is fuelling rising energy consumption, which increased by 4.6 per cent in 2017 and is expected to continue to grow at a rate of more than 4 per cent per year—faster than all the other major global economies.

India is taking a lead role in addressing climate change. For example, it is—

- Setting an ambitious renewable energy target to install 175 GW of capacity by 2022, up from 17 GW in 2016.

- Bringing about necessary structural reforms and promoting the right kind of business environment, through initiatives such as 'Startup India' and the 'Atal Innovation Mission'.

The government is also working hard to ensure that as many people as possible benefit from India's economic development. That means fostering growth across all sectors of the economy, supported by advancing technology, as well as policies to make economic growth inclusive.

THE RESOURCE POTENTIAL FOR INDIA IN THE ENERGY TRANSITION

India has significant indigenous hydrocarbons as well as wind, solar, hydro and biomass resources. If these are harnessed effectively, BP estimates they could enable the country to deliver its share of the International Energy Agency's carbon budget, consistent with the 2-degrees scenario (2DS), at a lower cost per tonne of CO_2 than many other major economies. Hence, India has the opportunity to be a leader in the energy transition, enabled by technology and policy choices.

Gas: BP estimates a domestic gas resource potential of more than 100 trillion cubic feet (TCF), which includes conventional, unconventional and yet-to-find resources. Together with upside from technology advancement, this resource base could meet up to 50 per cent of demand through 2050.

Oil: BP estimates that the application of enhanced recovery techniques in India's oil fields could yield an additional four billion barrels, both onshore and offshore, almost doubling current reserves.

Renewables: There are large untapped solar and wind resources in India which have the potential to be exploited at costs that are becoming increasingly competitive with fossil fuels. The opportunity to use biomass in a modern way, through conversion to gas, liquid fuels or power is significant and has the added benefit of improving air quality.

Coal: India has a material resource of indigenous coal (albeit low quality), which is expected to continue to play a significant, although declining, role in the energy mix.

INDIA'S CHANGING ENERGY MIX

The energy transition in India is already under way, unlocking exciting opportunities for business. India was the fifth-largest contributor to the global growth in renewables in 2017 and is seeing impressive growth in its solar and wind generation.

Our analysis shows the cost of onshore wind and solar becoming competitive with coal and starting to displace it in the mix. The opportunity for offshore wind appears more limited, as does the potential for further growth in hydroelectric power. Renewables could grow to 35–50 per cent of primary energy supply by 2050.

Natural gas could increase its share of the fuel mix to around 15 per cent, whether carbon is constrained or not. The major growth opportunities for natural gas are in industry (for process heat and as a chemical feedstock), transport (as compressed natural gas [CNG] and liquefied natural gas [LNG]) and city-gas (for heating and cooking). New gas-fired power generation will face intense competition from renewables, although there is scope to leverage existing stranded assets for grid balancing.

Coal will continue to play an important role in the electrical generation mix by providing grid balancing, as the proportion of renewables in the mix grows.

PRIORITY AREAS FOR ATTENTION

Natural gas

Natural gas has much lower carbon intensity per unit of energy than coal. Gas substitution also offers significant benefits for air quality through reduction of airborne particulates and pollutants such as nitrogen and sulphur oxides. In the long term, natural gas can be decarbonized to produce hydrogen as an energy vector—using the so-called carbon capture, use and storage (CCUS)—although there is little call for this before 2050 under the 2DS scenario for India.

Developing India's domestic gas production will help reduce energy imports, improving energy security as well as enabling more investment and creating jobs.

> India was the fifth-largest contributor to the global growth in renewables in 2017 and is seeing impressive growth in its solar and wind generation.

BOB DUDLEY ▸

BP is partnering with Reliance Industries to develop new offshore gas projects in India that we expect to bring online in the next few years. This will increase India's gas production by 25-30 per cent from current levels.

Natural gas resources must be developed responsibly, so that emission of methane to the atmosphere is minimized. Methane has a shorter lifetime in the atmosphere than carbon dioxide, but it has a higher global warming potential.

Renewables

Given India's significant onshore wind and solar resources, these could be harnessed to displace coal in electricity generation. By 2050, onshore wind could offer the lowest cost of supply, even when taking into account integration costs.

The potential for biomass conversion at scale is material, but transitional incentives may be required. India has already begun to encourage biogas production and new business models need to be created to incentivize the collection, sorting and aggregation of biomass to enable scale to be created.

Transport

Electrification of the vehicle fleet and substitution of liquid fuels with CNG or LNG are significant themes for India.

BP's analysis indicates that light-duty electric car costs (on a total cost of ownership basis) could converge with conventional vehicles from 2035 and that electric two- and three-wheel vehicles are close to cost parity today. CNG is already competitive in medium and heavy-duty vehicles and LNG is attractive for long-distance trucking. The electrification of buses, which follow established routes in urban areas, could become cost-competitive by 2030.

Vehicle weight and duty-cycle are key factors for the cost-effectiveness of transport electrification. Battery swapping, as well as fast, ultra-fast and flash charging will improve the business case and new business models will be required to cover upfront capital outlay.

New infrastructure will be required for any mode shift in transport.

Digitalization

Digital transformation is a major driver for change, which impacts how energy is produced, distributed and consumed. Digital technology has the potential to optimize energy systems, increasing efficiency. BP estimates that it could reduce current demand in India by around 18 per cent by 2050.

BP'S COMMITMENT TO INDIA

The energy industry is going through a period of great change. Demand is growing at a dramatic rate, mostly centred on rapidly expanding emerging economies. India accounted for 12 per cent of global growth in energy consumption in 2017.

India will continue to play a significant role in shaping global energy markets as they adapt to shifting supply and demand patterns, consumer preferences, policy environments and technological advances.

BP's relationship with India dates back more than a hundred years and we are now one of the largest international companies in India, employing around 7,500 people in the country across our businesses. We are constantly looking to build new partnerships and strengthen existing ones.

BP's upstream strategy for India is based on sustaining

production from existing declining fields, pursuing development of discovered resources, managing focused exploration and accessing a growing gas market.

We have a strategic alliance with Reliance Industries Limited (RIL) which combines BP's world-class deepwater exploration and development capabilities with RIL's project management and operations expertise. In 2017, we agreed to expand our partnership for strategic cooperation on new opportunities across India's energy sector.

We will jointly explore options to develop differentiated fuels, mobility and advanced low carbon energy businesses in India as the country transitions to a low-carbon world. We hope to collaborate in both conventional transport and aviation fuels retailing as well as on new mobility solutions, addressing electrification, digitalization and disruptive mobility trends.

Our Castrol lubricants brand has been in India since the early twentieth century and now has the largest manufacturing and distribution network in the country. Castrol has three manufacturing plants in India and a network of 350 distributors who sell to consumers and customers through over 100,000 retail outlets.

Lightsource BP, one of the world's leading solar developers and operators, is also establishing strong links with the country. Last year, it announced the completion of its first utility solar asset to be commissioned in India. The company also announced a joint venture with Everstone Group in India, to manage the Green Growth Equity Fund, which aims to bring up to $1 billion dollars of investment through contracted power, distribution infrastructure and energy services.

▸ ENERGIZING INDIA

BP'S GLOBAL COMMITMENT TO HELP ADVANCE THE ENERGY TRANSITION

The world's rising demand for energy is a real opportunity to expand our business and deliver higher returns for our investors.

Our aim is to do this through a strategy informed by the dual challenge of producing and delivering more energy in new ways with fewer emissions. We aim to do this by reducing emissions in our operations, improving our products and services to help our customers reduce their emissions, and by creating low carbon businesses as well as expanding our renewables operations. We call this our Reduce, Improve, Create framework.

> Developing India's domestic gas production will help reduce energy imports, improving energy security as well as enabling more investments and creating jobs.

To support our commitment to advance a low carbon future we have set ourselves tough near-term targets and aims. These include holding net growth in operational emissions flat out to 2025 against 2015 levels, while at the same time growing our business. We also plan to make 3.5 million tonnes of sustainable greenhouse gas emission reductions globally in our operations by 2025, which our operating businesses aim to deliver through improved energy efficiency, reduced flaring, and fewer methane emissions. Our methane intensity target will help ensure gas can play a full role in the energy transition. And to ensure that as our business grows, our carbon footprint does not, we will offset any net increase in our direct emissions above 2015 levels that is not covered by our sustainable reductions activity.

With 80 to 90 per cent of CO_2 emissions from oil and gas products coming from their use by consumers in power plants, transportation, industries and buildings, we are always looking for ways to improve our products—making them more efficient, producing biofuels and investing in new technologies to boost efficiency—to help consumers lower their emissions.

This article has set out the advantages of natural gas and how BP is producing more natural gas and plans to do so in India. We are also improving our fuels and lubricants for transport, and the petrochemicals products used to make everyday items as diverse as paints, clothes and packaging. Finally, we are investing significantly in growing our renewables businesses.

CONCLUSIONS

The dual challenge is one of the most serious issues the world faces and India is playing a crucial role in meeting it. We welcome India's commitment to helping solve this challenge, looking to meet the energy needs of its people while playing its part in reducing carbon emissions.

This is not dependent on any one big technological breakthrough. The world actually already has the know-how, resources, technology and, increasingly, the will to achieve this. But the challenges are too great for any one country or company. Everyone, from consumers to corporations to governments, needs to take responsibility

We see significant opportunities for India:

Energy transition

- India could position itself as a leader in the energy transition, leveraging renewables, gas and digital technologies and through policy choices to address the 'dual challenge'.

Resource base

- There are large renewable resources with potential to be exploited and opportunities to expand oil and gas resources via enhanced recovery technology and new exploration.

Role of gas

- Gas is becoming increasingly competitive in industry (for heat and as a feedstock), for city-gas applications and for transport—including CNG for light-duty vehicles and LNG for heavy-duty vehicles.

Air quality

- Levers to improve urban air quality include a greater uptake of gas, renewable power, re-purposing of biomass via conversion technology and electrification of transport in the long-term.

Nobody knows exactly what success will look like in the future. However, pursuing these opportunities will enable the following government policy objectives: increasing access to energy at affordable prices, improving security and independence, ensuring greater sustainability; and fostering economic growth.

As Prime Minister Modi said, 'We walk together, we move together, we think together, we resolve together, and together we take this country forward.'

12

POWERING THE US–INDIA ENERGY RELATIONSHIP

Nisha Biswal

US–India energy cooperation is positioned to be one of the fastest growing areas of the strategic and commercial relationship over the next twenty years. While the US is still listed as the fastest oil consuming nation in the world and India works fiercely to build out its capacity to meet its still growing domestic demands, both countries are pursuing all-of-the-above energy strategies that are focused on increasing energy access and energy security both domestically and abroad. This includes pursuing diversification of energy resources, supporting advancement of energy technology in relation to both renewable and non-renewable sources, and increasing the focus on the Indo-Pacific region as a hub for trade.

Energy cooperation has long played an important role in the bilateral relationship, touching nearly all aspects of the broader strategic partnership. Since 2005, the US and India have engaged in a productive bilateral energy dialogue and over the past decade that dialogue has expanded to include multiple government agencies, national labs, universities and other stakeholders. Year after year, the portfolio of partnerships and programmes to increase our energy cooperation grew to include research and development programmes in building efficiency, joint partnerships between the US and India-based companies in the oil and gas industry, applications and development of retrofitting technology for the power sector, new technology and storage solutions for renewable energy, resource management technology to bolster sustainable growth, clean coal investment, civil nuclear cooperation and programmes in multilateral fora such as Mission Innovation and the Clean Energy Ministerial.

The importance of energy cooperation and the desire to increase collaboration has been a priority sustained through several US and Indian administrations. The strategic and commercial role of energy between our two countries was reaffirmed and elevated during President Trump and Prime Minster Modi's 2017 meeting in Washington, when the two leaders announced the US–India strategic energy partnership. In order for both countries to achieve deeper and more meaningful cooperation, the US–India strategic energy partnership holds the stated goal of facilitating increased industry and stakeholder engagement, for which the US–India Business Council (USIBC) is a proud partner. As USIBC board member and Senior Vice President of Marketing for Tellurian Inc., Amos Hochstein comments, 'Within the global energy context, India is the most exciting market in the world. Prime Minister Modi's commitment to leading a transformation to a cleaner energy future and cleaner air throughout India, by substantially increasing the share of renewables and natural gas in India's energy mix, is a catalyst for investment and innovation. The impressive levels of investment by the government and the private sector are creating the opportunity for strengthening US–India ties.'

India's economic and strategic influence in the Indo-Pacific region continues to grow. During the launch of the Indo-Pacific

Business Forum at the US Chamber of Commerce in Washington, DC in July 2018, energy and energy infrastructure were highlighted as priorities by Secretary of State Pompeo and Secretary of Energy Rick Perry. Unveiled during the event, the US Government showed its own commitment to the region through the roll-out of the Asia EDGE (Enhancing Development and Growth through Energy) programme which will invest approximately $50 million to strengthen energy security and promote energy access across the region. As Asia EDGE and other Indo-Pacific initiatives are further developed by the US Government, private sector players of both countries will be essential to closing the investment gap and providing input to policymakers in order to continue growth for priority initiatives. The USIBC, a key partner in the Indo-Pacific Business Forum, is committed to providing industry input to help determine priority initiatives and facilitate US and Indian private sector opportunities for growth in our respective countries and throughout the Indo-Pacific region.

SECTOR OPPORTUNITIES

India has emerged as the fastest growing major economy in the world and is expected to account for about a quarter of the growth in global energy demand through 2040—offering enormous opportunities for US businesses to play a critical role in developing the energy sources and infrastructure India will need to achieve its goals.

While India and the US share all-of-the-above energy strategies and a focus on energy security, for India this is largely focused on 24×7 access to reliable energy. To meet these targets, India has focused on building out cleaner fuel sources including natural gas, renewable energy and civil nuclear energy. While some of the renewable buildout is ambitious, the vision for India is supported by abundant domestic solar and wind resources, a strong national government commitment to deployment of cleaner energy and technologies, an expanding building sector and a growing workforce. The widespread public concern with sustaining economic growth while improving quality of life metrics like air quality and a stable energy grid support the further development of these alternative fuel sources.

India's rapidly growing renewables market is also primed for US exports, with the US commerce department ranking India as the third most attractive market for US renewable energy exports. Despite the challenges posed by local content requirements and competition from companies with foreign government backing, hundreds of millions of dollars will be invested in the Indian renewable energy sector in the coming years. US companies are well placed to lead in this sector and play a key role in developing best practices and standards.

Energy efficiency is another area of opportunity for increased bilateral trade and cooperation. With roughly 80 per cent of India's commercial buildings yet to be built, robust implementation of energy efficiency policies that are in sync with US and global standards can help curb energy use and improve reliability, while still creating markets for innovative building technology services. Industrial energy efficiency, particularly in manufacturing, is an area ripe for more cooperation. Space cooling and efficient appliances will benefit from increased commercial ties and research and development (R&D). The USIBC supports mechanisms to promote out-of-the-box thinking for new development and deployment of cutting-edge technologies in the air conditioner industry—a market that will continue to grow in India with the burgeoning middle class and corporate campus development. Cooperation in energy efficiency has already supported the development and implementation of India's energy efficient building codes.

Fossil fuels will remain a significant source of energy for India and the region in the coming years. While the costs associated with the long shipping distance to India limit the competitiveness of US coal exports relative to suppliers in other countries, there is significant potential for increased US coal exports, as well as selling big-ticket mining equipment and continuing consultancy on mine safety and environmental issues. Increased cooperation in this area would create the potential for US technology and service providers not only to contribute to the efforts, which increase efficiency and reliability of existing coal power generation and implement clean coal technology, but also to have a real impact on India's emissions and air quality concerns.

> India has emerged as the fastest growing major economy in the world and is expected to account for about a quarter of the growth in global energy demand through 2040.

The recent increase in oil and gas sales between the US and India is another trend likely to continue over the next several years. India's growing import volume of US crude comes as it seeks to diversify sources with strong potential for cooperation on strategic petroleum reserves between the two countries.

Gas will be a particularly interesting area to watch. India's stated goal of increasing the share of gas to 15 per cent in the near term, and the focus on infrastructure and policy reforms in the gas sector, provide ample opportunities for growth—which the USIBC supports through its Executive Committee for Energy and Environment. Gas will also play an essential role in achieving India's renewable energy targets by providing increased flexibility for grid integration. The US is well positioned to become a key partner in this area whether it is through new exports to India, technology exchange or collaboration through the exchange of regulatory best practices.

Innovation is a particularly important component of both countries' energy strategies with technical collaboration in areas like smart grids, energy storage, energy efficiency, fossil fuel technologies and electric vehicles (EVs) poised to expand over the coming decades. The bilateral relationship provides opportunities for growth through both private enterprise and joint R&D programmes like the partnership to advance clean energy's new energy storage and smart grid track, which could be expanded to include clean coal and civil nuclear cooperation.

India's ambitious agenda for EVs is another area ripe for increased commercial ties and cooperation. As one of India's largest programmes, EV promotion enjoys government-wide support including, battery manufacturing industries and charging infrastructure. In September 2018, Prime Minister Modi outlined his vision for India's mobility development, focused on the 'Seven Cs' of mobility—common, connected, convenient, congestion-free, charged, clean and cutting-edge. Successful development of a competitive EV market in India will require engaging other countries and adopting global best practices suited for the Indian context.

These technological transformations would also have the benefit of reducing demand for energy imports and increasing India's energy security through resource diversification. Developing a cleaner and smarter grid alongside a growing number of EVs will be a challenge for India, requiring significant transformation of existing industries like automobile and battery manufacturing, as well as making changes to electricity generation and transmission regulations. In all these areas, India and the US can partner on regulatory and technology development while promoting continued business collaboration and advancing new investments.

BUILDING THE FUTURE

Energy is at the root of economic growth and has the potential to be the bright spot of the strategic and commercial relationship between the US and India. By promoting best practices and market-based solutions for the full spectrum of opportunities in the energy sector, the USIBC is displaying its excitement at being part of this growing partnership and to serve as the direct link between businesses, states and government in the US–India energy corridor. Continuing to lay the groundwork for future energy collaboration will enrich and support all pillars of the strategic relationship. This includes the goals of job growth—to serve India's young population, entering the market—and the continued growth of the industrial manufacturing sector by providing an energy grid known for stability.

Let's not forget that the benefits of increased energy cooperation goes both ways. Indian investment in the US energy infrastructure is growing and further linking our countries as partners in energy trade and innovation. India has made significant investments in the gas and renewable energy sectors in the US—and is looking to increase these investments massively.

One of India's largest and most ambitious programmes, EV promotion enjoys government-wide support for the country's EV and battery manufacturing industries, charging infrastructure and energy sector development.

As investment in the US and Indian energy industries grows, a significant and powerful role exists for subnational collaboration and partnerships in innovation. The potential of state-to-state engagements will not only help increase commercial ties and provide a platform for transparency but will also facilitate an increased exchange of best practices and standards. With our two nations sharing all-of-the-above energy strategies to achieve energy access and security in our shared Indo-Pacific region, it is important we continue to pursue strong collaboration at both a subnational and national level for the continued health of both countries.

13

THE 'DIGITAL OPERATIONS' IMPERATIVE FOR THE OIL, GAS AND CHEMICALS INDUSTRY IN INDIA

Ashwin Jacob

INTRODUCTION

Industry 4.0, coupled with the financialization of the world over the last two decades, has changed the mode of operations of the oil, gas and chemicals (OGC) industry globally. The continued increase in volatility in commodity prices, the electrification of transportation and the need for alternate fuels and renewables is rapidly shaping the role of OGC in society. As a result of the decades of operational challenges faced by the industry in the past, yield maximization, optimizing asset availability and utilization and reducing energy and maintenance costs are likely to become even more essential as industry participants strive to remain relevant. These challenges are likely to get accentuated with increasingly sophisticated expectations from customers (business-to-business [B2B], business-to-business-to-consumer [B2B2C] and business-to-consumer [B2C]), as well as a 'digital native' talent market that views the industry as 'old world'.

While there have been interesting developments in 'digital disruptor technologies' across industries, their application in the OGC industry needs to be looked at in the context of industry maturity and imperatives.

Industry 4.0 has further unleashed a whole spectrum of digital interventions that not only span the new world industries, but are now starting to make a series of changes to the old world industries as the lines between them are blurring—marking the fact that true convergence may be upon us. Digital is driving a number of changes, both in the products and services of industries and in the means of consumption by both B2B and B2C consumers—with an increased focus on societal disruptions.

Industry and its select challenges	Technology disruptions
Transportation: Changed mobility preferences, customer shift to electric vehicles, shared mobility a norm, fuel price volatility	• Sharing economy • Electric vehicles • Autonomous vehicles • Connected vehicles expanding on telematics
Banking: Economic liberalization and changing customer preferences	• Biometrics • Distributed ledgers/Fintech • Hyper-connected and always online
Construction: Smart cities are focusing on comprehensively improving occupant lives	• Sustainable materials • Improved collaborative technologies • Mass customization
Healthcare: Government interventions on drug pricing, medical tourism and telehealth	• Personalized healthcare • Telehealth and distributed diagnosis • Improved data storage and smart sensors

Media and entertainment: Video-on-demand, content streaming and hyper-targeted content and advertising	• Cloud video providers • Pay per use/Pay per view • Social listening
Manufacturing: Operational excellence, commodity price pressures and talent retention	• Augmented Internet of Things (IoT) • Cloud-enabled analytics platform • Robotic process automation (RPA)

Figure 1: Industry and technology disruptions
Source: *Deloitte analysis*

OGC industry observers know that this industry has been 'digital' for decades. Advanced process controls (APC) and distributed control systems (DCS) operations with real-time optimization capability leveraging data from plant instruments are not new. The implications of convergence between operating technology (OT) and information technology (IT) are also different for this industry as it had been one of the early adopters of IT–OT integration.

The industry started the journey early, enhancing their transactional capabilities with 'system of records' applications offered by large enterprise resource planning (ERP) softwares as well as data historians. It has since evolved to a 'system of differentiation' focus with specialized industry applications offering functional excellence with simulation and optimization engines. This resulted in a fairly sophisticated focus on 'data analytics'— often stand-alone spreadsheet-like decision support applications— which focused on drawing insights from the wealth of information available in underlying applications. Thus analytics, or digital twins in some form or shape, are not 'net-new' to this industry. Despite these technologies enhancing value realization, the industry finds itself at a stage today where it is perceived to be a laggard in adopting emerging digital technologies.

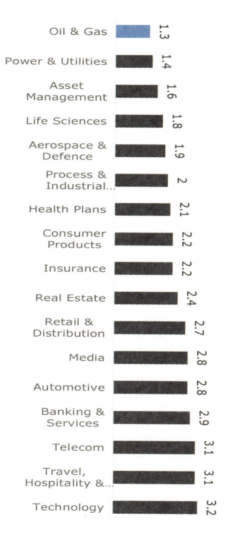

Figure 2: Average Digital Maturity by Sector

Note: *Companies in S&P 100 respectively ranked on digital maturity using Deloitte's Digital Maturity Index (DMI) framework. Monitor Deloitte developed the DMI based on a study of the digital capabilities of the S&P 100 companies.*
Source: *eMarketer, Nielsen, Monitor Deloitte analysis*

As seen in Figure 2, oil and gas companies rank lowest in digital maturity among all the other industries studied in S&P 100. The size of assets distributed across geographies and developed over a course of time, and a focus on safety, have led to a multitude of technologies being adopted by OGC companies.

THE 'BURNING PLATFORM' IN AN INDIAN CONTEXT

Going forward, sustaining India's average GDP growth of over 7 per cent will need large amounts of energy. From 754 million tonnes of oil equivalent (mtoe) in 2017, it is expected that India's primary energy demand will almost double to ~1,365 mtoe by 2030.

Among the large economies, India's demand for energy is expected to increase the most. It is expected that a major proportion of this—nearly 33 per cent—will be contributed by oil and gas. At the same time, India has seen a rapid evolution of its alternate energy policy, which has resulted in the adoption of alternate energy sources in power as well as some early movement in electric vehicle (EV) adoption. However, it is expected that in the middle-term, India will continue to be largely dependent on hydrocarbons for a significant portion of its energy demands for transportation.

India is highly import-dependent for its energy requirements, with oil and gas (O&G) imports constituting ~23 per cent of its overall import basket. Therefore, with its burgeoning demand, India will need to continue to maximize efficiencies across its OGC sector to minimize the cost to the consumer—else there could be a real risk to sustaining the growth story of the nation.

The country is also going through a consumption cycle uptick with a rapidly growing per capita income. This indicates that the chemical sector in India also has excellent demand prospects in the near- to medium-term future. This sector has been growing at over 10 per cent since 2010 and is likely to continue the momentum over the next decade as well.

Use of petrochemicals (~10 per cent compound annual growth rate [CAGR] for 2014–17) derived from oil and gas is becoming increasingly ubiquitous in the country. As with the developed world, petrochemicals provide the majority of materials that we utilize daily—such as its use in packaging, clothing and detergents. One change that is being seen on a global basis as electrification disrupts the scale and size of transportation fuels is that a number of companies are looking at increased conversion to chemicals from crude as a means to sustain business. This is also expected to happen in the Indian context—for instance, the Ratnagiri complex is being developed as a world-scale refinery and petrochemical complex with the flexibility to change its configuration.

> India has seen a rapid evolution of its alternate energy policy, which has resulted in the adoption of alternate energy sources in power.

The domestic chemical sector is also expected to grow by about 12 per cent annually up to 2030 with increased demand from end-use industries such as textiles, automotive, personal care, construction chemicals and agrochemicals as well as in application-driven segments such as surfactants, paints, performance-enhancing chemicals, coatings and colorants.

Another important aspect of the Indian oil sector is the imbalance between finished oil products and domestic upstream production leading to heavy dependence on imported crude oil—with refinery configurations making it unattractive to operate at a poor sweet–sour differential. This necessitates the requirement of being able to operate with unconventional means with greater agility.

India, therefore, needs to consider ways to enhance domestic production, improve efficiencies and bring in world-class technologies and product development capabilities, in order to capitalize on market opportunity. Given the global nature of the industry, the Indian OGC sector could consider embracing digital interventions across the value chain in order to protect its positions in the Indian market and enhance its share of the global market. Today, integration of technologies enables faster, safer and cheaper production on the part of companies. As mentioned earlier, the OGC sector does not seem to have taken full advantage of a world tending towards infinite computing capabilities in order to react in an increasingly nimble manner to asset and market conditions—and other externalities—to drive safe, profitable operations. The nature of margins and profitability in the OGC sector has sometimes tended to be a challenge to adopting these emerging disruptors for fear of impacting production or disturbing the status quo of operations—given that yields of over 95 per cent have already been achieved. This, however, does not mean that a number of digital disruptors cannot be considered across the OGC sector in areas such as commercial services and share services, to transform and drive the enterprise to an efficiency frontier that conventional ERP and other package software solutions are unable to provide today. The visibility and clarity which is brought about by digital technologies and advanced analytics can help provide unprecedented granular insight into operations, increase agility and support better decision-making. Digital enablers, from process digitization to robotics and automation, can also help unlock potential by supporting processes in dynamic ways. Indian OGC players, therefore, need to explore, identify and imbibe leading industry practices for many of these digital interventions, in order to stay competitive in the marketplace.

DIGITAL DISRUPTORS IN THE OGC CONTEXT

Digital disruptor technologies are a new set of tools in the armouries of corporations as they look to innovate, understand the market, improve efficiency and turn data into insights and—eventually—margins. The disruptors also present an opportunity for an 'old-world' industry such as OGC to take a step into the new world of selling products and services digitally, thereby driving industry convergence—albeit in the reverse direction. Advancements in underlying technology, coupled with the falling cost of adoption and increasing connectivity, are providing newer opportunities to innovate. These are also creating disruptive changes in traditional business functions and forcing companies to rethink their future strategies. Some of the key technologies shown in Figure 3 are becoming mainstream and changing the way organizations envisage their future:

Taking advantage of these 'RADICALS' requires commitment and, often, significant investment. As an illustration—building from a base of IoT to create a truly 'smart' factory requires exploring a strategy that includes synergies with other 'exponential technologies' such as additive manufacturing, mixed reality and

Figure 3: The disruptors
Source: *Deloitte analysis*

many others—in order to incorporate a broad range of capabilities into a revised manufacturing model.

However, today these 'RADICALS' seem to be primarily in a testing stage in the OGC industry, largely in the fashion of a science experiment. For example, a combination of IoT and analytics can help in improving asset reliability. Currently, manual inspection of external and internal corrosion during routine inspections is a major effort and any oversight in these potential inspections can lead to major, costly breakdowns or even hazards. However, the increasing usage of sensors throughout the assets along with deep learning analytical models to leverage historical data can potentially transform this area and significantly increase asset integrity. This solution helps to identify very low risk corrosion areas, where inspection effort can be drastically reduced. For the areas that are identified to be at higher risk of corrosion, the frequency of inspection and targeted action can be proportionately increased. The sensors have the potential to minimize human error during inspection while the analytics help draw focus to the right areas in the asset.

In the OGC context, some of these 'RADICALS' are likely to become more important than the rest and have an opportunity to impact the industry significantly.

DIGITAL TRANSFORMATION IN THE OGC INDUSTRY

The imperative for the Indian OGC industry, therefore, stems from both the macro forces impacting the underlying industry as well as the opportunities that present themselves on account of developments pertaining to the digital disruptors.

Organizations also need to decide on the areas of interventions for digital innovations. Organizations may choose to focus on different aspects of the value chain to kick-start their digital journey. The choice will depend on the organizations' level of comfort with the technology, the investment required and the benefit potential. The areas of interventions can be divided into four broad categories (see Figure 4).

In our view, the way for the industry to seize the day is by driving digital transformation efforts to enhance their agility and collaborative capabilities for prompt decision-making.

For many multinational corporations, operations span multiple silos that operate with inconsistent information dispersed across fragmented applications and processes. Yet, in asset-intensive process industries, operations (comprising production, logistics, asset management and customer management) form the part of their value chain that has the highest impact on profitability. Unlocking value from operations is one of the best ways to address profitability challenges in a competitive market.

> The domestic chemical sector is also expected to grow by about 12 per cent annually up to 2030 with increased demand from end-use industries such as textiles, automotive, personal care, construction chemicals and agrochemicals.

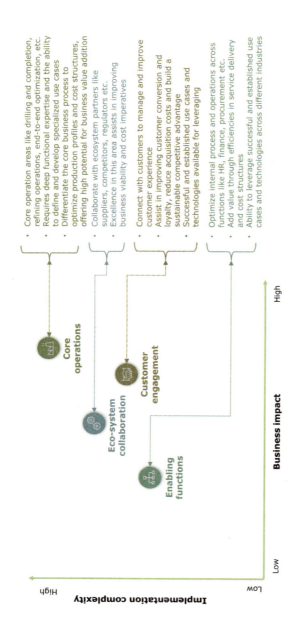

Figure 4: Key areas of intervention

Source: Deloitte analysis

Figure 5: Path to digital transformation

Source: *Deloitte analysis*

Organizations today	Organizations tomorrow
Multiple, niche approaches through local improvement activities	Holistic focus across the value chain optimizing and addressing changing market context across multiple plants and functions in a coherent and dynamic way
Poor integration of information across the enterprise decision-making within departments in isolation	Collaboration, real-time information and speed of decisions drive value
Plan and react	Plan, predict, prevent and optimize
Value improvements that rely on individual's knowledge and experience	Integrated platforms, data, applications and processes enable consistent sharing of common, real-time
Delayed insights across the value chain limit response to market opportunity	

Figure 6: Organizations of today versus tomorrow

Source: Deloitte analysis

Some examples of digital interventions across the OGC value chain for organizations of the future are given below:

Segment	Value Driver	Indicative Digital Interventions
Upstream	Efficient oil and gas production	• Dynamic sensor-driven geological analysis to identify reserves • Machine learning to improve oil recovery • Robotizing platforms to improve safety • Augmented/Virtual reality (AR/VR) for remote visualization of rig operations

Segment	Value Driver	Indicative Digital Interventions
Midstream and Storage	More uptime and faster turnaround	• IOT Sensors for condition monitoring • AR/VR for remote visualization of asset health • Dynamic demand-based nomination and flow management • Distributed ledger enablement for consumption of the midstream
Manufacturing and Processing	Cost-efficient operations	• Real time predictive analytics to optimize asset operations • Artificial Intelligence to optimize feedstock choices on a real time basis • Predicting asset failures to facilitate preventive maintenance • Dynamic always-on barrier management to protect the physical and cyber integrity of the asset • Preventive maintenance to reduce human interventions and optimize maintenance shutdowns
B2B	Predictable supply chains	• Blockchain-enabled contracting for transparency and quick decision making • Real time assessment of risks in demand and supply of all types • Dynamic rerouting of product based on live demand signals
		• Route optimization to drive milk run delivery efficiency • Differentiated customer experience enabled by AR/VR to validate product fit for application • Dynamic pricing driven by market intelligence to capture and maximize value from price arbitrage

▸ ENERGIZING INDIA

Segment	Value Driver	Indicative Digital Interventions
B2C	Tapping consumer preferences and providing consumer conveniences	• Applications to provide consumer a one-stop solution to all energy needs • Engaging with retail outlets to provide customized offers

Figure 7: Digital interventions for OGC organizations of tomorrow
Source: Deloitte analysis

Tomorrow's organizations are expected to work across value chains and functions to optimize the entire operation, which could be represented by the following graphics:

TODAY'S BUSINESS: VALUE CHAIN SILOS

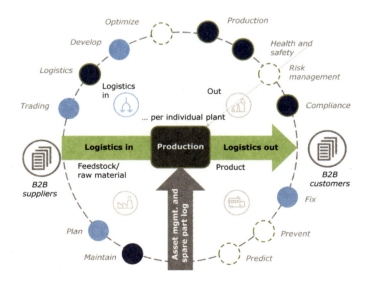

DIGITAL OPERATIONS

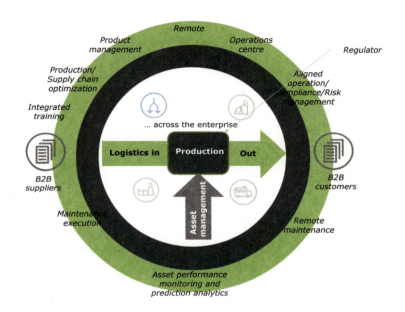

Figure 8: Silos to integrated digital operations
Source: *Deloitte analysis*

However, the journey towards digitization is not simple and straight-forward. There are several changes that an organization will have to undertake while trying to succeed in its digital journey.

KEY CRITERIA FOR A SUCCESSFUL JOURNEY TO THE FUTURE

The key success criteria broadly fall into the three areas of technology: architecture, organization and governance and people.

Technology architecture: The technology architecture and its components are expected to continue to evolve and revolutionize the way we work. In light of this, two key areas that need to be considered are:

- Strong integration—Unlike at the enterprise level, where there are typically a handful of applications, the operations system level is made up of a multitude of highly specialized applications that need to 'talk' to each other efficiently.
- Good data governance—Data-driven insights are critical to digital operations and must be seen as valuable strategic assets. Hence, a strong data governance framework is needed to assure all stakeholders that data is easily, safely, quickly and reliably available.

Organization and governance: To achieve digital operations, one will need to consider the following key areas from an organization and governance perspective.

- Flexible organization structure—In a future where information is available everywhere and at anytime, the traditional 'command and control' structure may no longer apply. Analytics can provide contextual insights—and recommend actions to be taken—directly to the connected plant worker. Therefore, in the future, the plant worker may have the ability to make informed decisions without the need to wait for instructions from his supervisors. Decision-making is expected to be faster and come from people who best know the situation on the ground. To enable this, tomorrow's organization structure will have to be flexible to allow for greater autonomy for the plant worker. Thus, standard reporting and performance objectives may have to

be looked at from a the perspective of a different kind of team-based operating model.
- A combined IT/OT organization—The agile asset of the future may have a single organization managing and operating IT and OT to maximize the benefits from IT/OT technology convergence.

People: With a more globalized workforce, the operations of the future need to consider using their skills for gain in productivity and innovation; different ways to attract and retain talent and use social platforms, mobility and gaming to enable engagement and learning.

The talent requirement priorities of the future connected plant operator are expected to change. First and foremost, he needs to be technology-savvy. With digital technologies giving him more decision-making autonomy, his understanding of the plant will also need to be broader-based, covering commercials, asset-reliability and so forth in addition to his primary knowledge of operating a plant.

The role of the future connected maintenance technician is also expected to change. As technologies continue to advance rapidly, the plant will become more and more automated, requiring fewer and fewer plant operators on-site.

BARRIERS AND CHALLENGES FOR DIGITAL ADOPTION

However, organizations will also have to overcome a number of barriers to succeed as digital organizations.

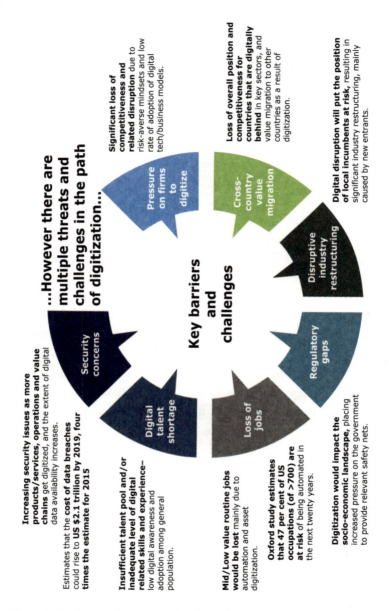

Figure 9: Barriers and challenges to digital transformation

Source: Deloitte analysis

Managements have different attitudes to digital transformations and select different transformation pathways. Broadly, we would categorize organizations which undertake such journeys into three archetypes—'Test and Watch', 'Planning a Transformation' and 'Commercial Use Case Adopters.'

Test and Watch: These organizations are early observers of digital technologies. A typical Test and Watch process would involve developing proofs of concept/technology demonstration pilots to solve clearly constructed problems. The general belief is that, based on the success of this proof of concept, the pilot could then be scaled up for commercial exploitation at an asset level and then at an organization level.

These companies make incremental gains by adopting this staged approach. The developmental focus is on testing multiple solutions—usually with low levels of management commitment. Since solutions are also developed incrementally—they take more time to be adopted across the organization. Unlike the legacy technology deployments where designs are completed and implemented, a 'digital with development and operations' (DevOps) mindset means the results are never perfect—rather, they need to be perfected. This uncertainty creates an increased inertia towards deployment in these companies. Therefore, their solutions are developed within a strict framework of time and effort and hence are cost efficient and solve simple problems.

Planning a Transformation: These, typically, are large organizations with significant investments already made in large enterprise applications. This sunk capital acts as an inertia towards change. They often embark on journeys to design the full spectrum of digital applications as it pertains to their existing stack of applications with the aim to define a full digital transformation. The emphasis is on exploring benchmarks/comparators as well as identifying applicability to their business.

Through such an approach, these companies hope to trigger an enterprise-wide re-imagining of their businesses and undertake transformations holistically involving all stakeholders without rushing into a specific solution to solve incremental problems. They would develop short-term, medium-term and long-term development plans. However, often stakeholder consultations and finalizing a single plan take longer than anticipated thus running the risk of having to wait for the right time to start.

Commercial Use Case Adopters: These organizations are focused on identifying specific business problems using commercially proven technologies. The emphasis is on robust integration of proven technologies, which are scaled-up to give them a disruptive advantage in their business operations. They may develop integrated proofs of concept (PoCs) to validate the business potential—to be implemented rapidly once proven.

Since these companies pick commercially proven technologies, they limit the risk of failures by focusing on integration of these technologies. However, they may miss development of new areas of value creation as they generally do not pick upcoming technologies. Similarly, since they don't undertake a holistic exercise, their gains are also expected to be limited to the areas of their business.

Most of the Indian industry falls under the 'Test and Watch' category.

THE CALL FOR ACTION

Digital operations are expected to drive operations of the future. However, just 'doing' digital things is not likely to make an organization more digital. To be digital and to lead digital disruption, organizations would need to embark on a journey of 'being' digital and blend digital capabilities with digital behaviors. It's the application of new mindsets that could enable organizations to leverage new technologies to their fullest potential.

1. Exploring digital: In this, organizations leverage traditional technologies to automate existing capabilities. The organization would be dabbling with different aspects of 'RADICALS' with little or no change to the organization itself.
2. Doing digital: Organizations start leveraging digital technologies to extend capabilities but are often siloed and still largely focused around current business, operating and customer models.
3. Becoming digital: Organizations leverage digital technologies to become more synchronized and less siloed—with more advanced changes to current business, operating, and customer models.
4. Being digital: Business, operating and customer models are leveraged for digital and are profoundly different from prior business, operating or customer models.

The organizations shall look at exhibiting and embracing different components of digital behaviour—what we call 'digital DNA'. These components represent a set of special traits and characteristics that position businesses to thrive in a digital world by helping create the optimal organizational environment for 'being' digital.

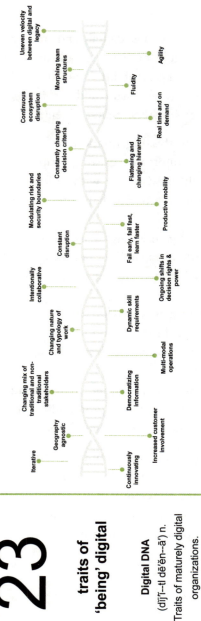

Figure 10: Digital DNA

Source: *Deloitte analysis*

However, this journey to 'being digital' is challenging and not easily defined. Organizations need to adopt an 'agile' approach characterized by iterative sprints to continuously drive digital impact. Agility enables rapid organizational learning by providing feedback loops based on results for deployment of incremental changes, and assists in responding to business changes, social shifts and technology advances. This approach empowers teams to self-organize and collaborate, to continuously approve and make fast and transparent decisions.

Each sprint in the agile approach is broken into three distinct phases:

1. **Imagine—look forward, explore broadly:** The idea is to explore customer needs, identify critical touch-points and experiences and study changing expectations to capture future-ready improvements. The in-depth discovery helps in shaping the next steps and prioritizing commitments. Evaluation of the organizational and configuration changes required also helps to prioritize the ambitions that need to become reality.
2. **Deliver—iteratively refine concepts, prototype, test, and plan:** In this phase, what organizations imagine begin to take shape. Ideas, designs, and technologies are tested against customer and stakeholder expectations for fitness and validity alongside their ability to surprise customers and stakeholders. This helps in refining concepts and plan for the future operating model necessary to drive to scale.
3. **Run—agile operations create business impact:** The digital business is built, launched, and deployed atop engagement platforms as the plans begin to drive the change envisioned. The business transformation takes shape, benefits begin to be realized at scale and the organization is prepared for continuous learning.

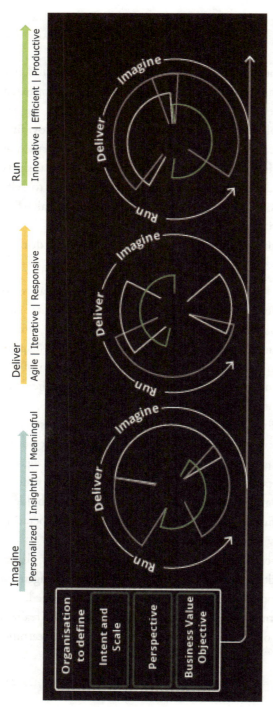

Figure 11: Agile approach to digital transformation

Source: Deloitte analysis

For the Indian industry, we believe players should change their approach from 'Test and Watch' to the agile approach for digital transformation. We believe that Indian players should adopt different approaches and select areas of interventions in their digital journey. The following figure highlights the approaches that Indian players could consider undertaking:

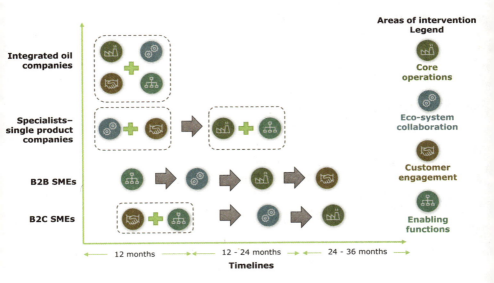

Figure 12: Sample pathways for Indian OGC companies

Source: Deloitte analysis

Large integrated companies can immediately adopt approaches similar to organizations that are 'Planning a Transformation', which could help them undertake enterprise-wide digital transformation.

Specialists or companies operating in a single value chain are already restricted in their operational coverage and hence, can focus on improving the ecosystem of suppliers and logistics—

along with customer focus—in the first year. The specialists can then subsequently analyze core and enabling operations for digital transformation opportunities.

Similarly, small and medium-size enterprises (SMEs) can undertake digital transformations similar to 'Commercial Use Case Adopters' that could solve problems and give quick results.

No matter what path OGC companies choose, it is imperative that they undertake digital transformations immediately for growth and survival.

REFERENCES

1 MOSPI–Official Website
2 *BP Energy Outlook 2018–India*
3 DGCI&S Kolkata, *Indian Express*, September 2018
4 Department of Chemical and Petrochemicals (MoCF)–Statistics and Monitoring Division
5 Department of Chemical and Petrochemicals (MoCF)–Statistics and Monitoring Division
6 *Economic Times*, May 2018, 'Specialty chemical sector may double market size by 2025'

14

PREPARING INDIA'S WORKFORCE FOR THE FOURTH INDUSTRIAL REVOLUTION

Subha Srinivasan and *Kumar Kandaswami*[1]

INTRODUCTION

The growth of India's current GDP stands at 7.3 per cent, with the International Monetary Fund (IMF) country report identifying India as one of the fastest growing economies in 2018–19 and 2019–20.[2]

Attributing the anticipated growth to enabling reforms and policies such as the goods and services tax (GST), inflation-targeting monetary policy frameworks, the Insolvency and Bankruptcy Code (IBC) and initiatives to improve Foreign Direct Investment (FDI) flows and the business climate, the economy is expected to sustain the growth momentum in the future. The high growth and the size of the economy,[3] contributing to 15 per cent global growth from a purchasing power parity (PPP) measure, highlights the country's potential to further reduce inequalities and take significant measures towards poverty alleviation.[4]

However, to sustain and channelize the growth engine,

leveraging the country's demographic dividend is essential. The country's growing working-age population (62 per cent) can work as an advantage by enabling the youth to acquire relevant skill sets to meet future requirements. This includes preparing them for the fourth industrial revolution (4IR) and additionally enhancing their adaptability to the future of work. Gaps in formal education (in terms of learning levels and drop-outs) and the current labour force participation rate (LFPR) (54 per cent),[5] compounded by the fact that only 5 per cent of Indians are considered formally skilled, present a scenario with both opportunities and challenges. The female LFPR is 50 per cent lower than the male LFPR[6] as women have limited access to skilling and 126 million people—constituting 95 per cent of the women employed—are in the informal sector.[7] A recent IMF report highlights that an increase in women's participation in the workforce, to the same extent as men, can increase India's GDP by 27 per cent.[8]

The Indian Government has increased its commitment to the manufacturing sector with digital initiatives such as Bharat Interface for Money (BHIM), Aadhaar-enabled payment system and direct benefits transfer. Influenced by the rapid changes of 4IR, business in India is experiencing shifts towards automation, big data and the Internet of Things (IoT) to drive productivity, innovation and efficiencies. This trend prioritizes the need to prepare the Indian workforce, by engaging businesses and communities, for the rapid evolution of technologies, shifts in the physical–digital interface and the changing nature of work. The government, through the National Skill Development Mission, aspires to train 400 million people by 2022 to address the skill gap in the country.[9] This presents an opportunity for the government, business and not-for-profit sectors to collaboratively shape the skilling narrative in India with high potential for economic and societal impact.

As the world prepares for 4IR—evolving from advances in computing to artificial intelligence, robotics, automation and other exponential technologies—it becomes important to analyse how one of the world's fastest growing economies is preparing its workforce to succeed in the revolution. This involves understanding the impact of the future of work on its working population and the environment in which the workforce will operate. It is in this context that certain measures to prepare the future working population for 4IR have been recommended in this article.

> A recent IMF report highlights that an increase in women's participation in the workforce, to the same extent as men, can increase India's GDP by 27 per cent.

EMERGENCE OF THE FOURTH INDUSTRIAL REVOLUTION

The term 4IR was framed by Klaus Schwab, the founder and chairman of the World Economic Forum, as an amalgamation of the physical, digital and biological worlds that will reshape the manner in which people and business interact with technology while transforming the future of work.[10] Schwab highlights that the advent of self-driving cars, supercomputing, robots and genetic modification should not take away the focus from humankind benefiting from the revolution and reducing inequalities. The

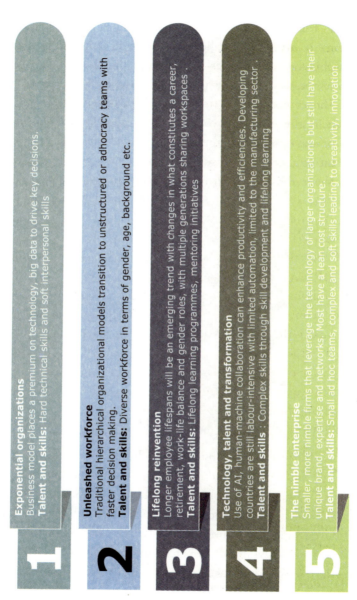

Figure 1

Source: *Deloitte report on the Evolution of Work, 2018*

transition from simple digitization (in the third industrial revolution) to disruptive innovation through a combination of digital technologies and platforms is changing the way companies do business across the manufacturing, services and agriculture sectors. The evolution of 4IR will be influenced by contextual prisms such as geography, gender, development status and local cultures or ways of life.

The introduction of new technologies and business models can, in turn, shape the kind of talent required, shifting the nature of work and the workforce. A recent report on the Evolution of Work describes emerging realities of the future of work across seventy-two influential forces, which are summarized in the figure below.[11] Some of the talent and skill sets that will enhance preparedness towards 4IR have also been outlined.

The additional influencing factors include ethics of work and society in terms of worker well-being, and regulating innovative business models that, at times, disrupt labour force participation in a traditional sector and bypass taxation and other laws in unregulated areas.[12] This specifically applies to developing economies that are labour intensive and where technology-driven models are perceived to be replacing human effort.

While the Indian Government and industry prepare for 4IR, a snapshot of global and regional preparedness across areas of focus for global executives—in terms of what they consider as successful factors to transition to 4IR—will provide useful insights in shaping the local agenda. In terms of potential societal impact, while there is overall optimism towards reducing inequalities from an Asia-Pacific (APAC) perspective, leaders in India anticipate social challenges and increased income inequality given the current education and skilling levels. In addition, 70 per cent APAC leaders believe automation will replace human labour.[13] However, a positive picture emerges from Deloitte's analysis of the 'seven new realities', wherein despite the technological disruptions, a new wave of human skill sets or talent is required which can enable higher levels of human-machine collaboration. Human skills are required to conduct complex tasks, customize support and manage machine integration, presenting a significant opportunity to introduce a range of skill development and lifelong learning initiatives.[14] In addition, the right talent has to be in place to drive 4IR with a distinctive set of technical skills and soft skills along with an ecosystem to support entrepreneurships and an environment that promotes diversity at the workplace.

INDIA PREPARING FOR 4IR

India stands to potentially reap the benefits of 4IR. However, the question is how prepared are the country's industries, government and communities for the shift in terms of strategy, technologies and talent and the societal impact that can be created? Daniel Pink, in his book *A Whole New Mind*, highlights that the world is gravitating from a knowledge economy to a conceptual age where skill—sets building on innovation, intuition, communication and collaboration will take precedence over rote learning, routine ways of doing work and textual understanding.[15] While India is transitioning towards industrial automation and digital transformation, the biggest challenge it faces, akin to Pink's predictions for developing economies, is the dearth of a skilled workforce that understands robotic technology, IoT or big data. As already mentioned, only 5 per cent of India's population is formally skilled—in comparison, China's skilled workforce makes up 24 per cent of its population.[16]

Gaps in formal education

The education system has traditionally been content focused, but

4IR predicts a skill-based future of work. Integrating technological education and digital literacy into the educational structure early on can help prepare generations for short-term employability and long-term skill readiness for the workforce. However, significant challenges have been faced across the education ecosystem, from high school dropout levels in middle and high school, poor enrolment in higher education and poor learning levels, which are outlined in the education challenge map in Figure 2.

The ASER Beyond Basics report captures the perceptions and the extent of workforce preparedness of 14–18-year-olds in rural India—49 per cent males and 76 per cent females have never used the internet; 60 per cent who want to pursue higher education cannot read a second grade text; only 43 per cent can solve a simple division problem and an entire cohort of youth have limited foundational reading and math abilities.[17] The report concludes that India's demographic dividend may not materialize if we do not invest in developing the knowledge, skills and opportunities for the youth to emerge as invested stakeholders in the workforce.[18]

From a higher education lens, countries like China have an engineering dividend approach to meeting their skilled worker targets for 4IR, with three million qualified engineering graduates and a 97 per cent employment rate. In contrast, a recent report highlighted that 95 per cent engineers in India are not sufficiently skilled for software development jobs; only 1.4 per cent of a sample of 36,000 engineering graduates could write functional and efficient code; and the All India Council for Technical Education (AICTE) has closed 410 engineering colleges between 2014 and 2018.[19,20,21] The current overall employability rate stands at 46 per cent, while only 52 per cent engineering graduates get a job after their course—highlighting the need to focus on stronger science, technology, engineering and math (STEM) initiatives in

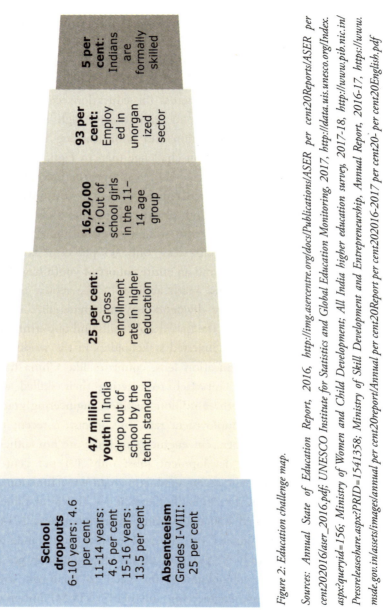

Figure 2: Education challenge map.

Sources: Annual State of Education Report, 2016, http://img.asercentre.org/docs/Publications/ASER per cent20Reports/ASER per cent202016/aser_2016.pdf; UNESCO Institute for Statistics and Global Education Monitoring, 2017, http://data.uis.unesco.org/Index.aspx?queryid=156; Ministry of Women and Child Development; All India higher education survey, 2017-18, http://www.pib.nic.in/PressreleaseShare.aspx?PRID=1541358; Ministry of Skill Development and Entrepreneurship, Annual Report, 2016-17, https://www.msde.gov.in/assets/images/annual per cent20report/Annual per cent202016-2017 per cent20- per cent20English.pdf

the Indian education sector. This will also align with business and the government's agenda to shape talent with complex or high skills for the workforce.

Employability of youth

A recently released Deloitte report jointly published with Global Business Coalition for Education signifies that, out of the 1.8 billion youth between the ages of 15 and 29, 61 per cent are living in Asia.[22] The Education Commission forecasts that 50 per cent of the two billion youth worldwide may be unprepared to join the workforce by 2030.[23] Globally, emerging technologies like artificial intelligence, robotics, automation and quantum computing, etc. will displace five million low- and middle-skill jobs.[24] As 1.3 million Indians enter the working-age population every month, 18.3 million Indians are currently unemployed.[25] Formal and non-farm payrolls account for only 34 per cent of jobs, and 90 per cent of the employment in agriculture and 70 per cent of the employment in non-agriculture sectors is in the unorganized sector.[26] The 2017–18 quarterly report on employment reveals that sectors like manufacturing (65 per cent), education (15 per cent), transport, trade and health have seen a positive change in terms of total employment, while sectors like construction have seen a negative change. The report also highlights the recent shifts in the nature of jobs, with a positive change in regular workers followed by contractual and casual workers.[27] While these are positive trends, the Ministry of Skill Development and Entrepreneurship (MSDE) report depicts a growing skill gap in sectors like construction, retail, electronics and IT-ITeS, beauty and wellness, handloom and handicrafts, and road transport and highways.[28]

Skill mapping to meet the requirements of 4IR

A recent study by the Observer Research Foundation (ORF) and the World Economic Forum (WEF) revealed that 70 per cent of the youth are not aware of government programmes and schemes on skill development and 51 per cent of the youth lack guidance on identifying jobs that can match their skill sets or type of skill sets that can be gained.[29] In this scenario, India has to harness the demographic dividend by strengthening the education ecosystem and repurposing the skill development agenda with a cross-gender focus, to create a viable, desirable and productive future of work for its youth. It is important to further study the aspirations of India's youth and the changing requirements of business to further align career ambitions and types of job opportunities.

Against this backdrop, the revolution brings to the fore two buckets of skill sets from an Indian perspective—higher- order and lower-order skills. In order to develop these two distinctive skill areas, it becomes increasingly critical to build strong initiatives aligned to SDG 4: Quality Education, and SDG 8: Inclusive and sustainable economic growth and employment for all.[30] Second, it is essential to define inclusive skill development programmes providing opportunities for the most underserved sections of the population to reskill or upskill, mitigating the danger 4IR poses in widening levels of social and economic inequality, etc. Third, given the complexity of 4IR, adopting a collaborative approach—as outlined in SDG 17: Partnership for goals—between government, business and communities enables higher levels of preparedness and more opportunities to create sustained impact.

PATHWAYS TO PREPARING THE YOUTH FOR 4IR

Education-linked opportunities

Addressing the gap in formal education through apprenticeship models can offer youth on-the-job skill development training while they are completing their higher education. This approach resonates with the government's aspiration to increase apprenticeship seats through the 2014 amendment to the Apprentices Act, 1961.[31] After school and out-of-school programmes are also suggested pathways to engage youth from the vulnerable and marginalized communities while they are still invested in the education ecosystem.[32] Scaling the National Vocational Education Qualification Framework (NVEQF) linked programmes at schools and universities could also be viable options to increase the number of skilled youth.

Skill development across the four skill categories

India has the distinctive advantage of an evolved skill development ecosystem owing to the presence of standardization in training levels through qualification frameworks (QPNOS) and industry-linked sector skill councils (SSCs) that are invested in strengthening the quality and impact of skilling programmes. The National Skill Development Corporation (NSDC), which comes under the MSDE, has over the years been a part of the growth of numerous skill training partners that have scaled up their initiatives across India. Currently, the NSDC has 428 training partners[33] with a pan-India outreach across 6,882 training centres. In addition, 1,105 job roles (qualification packs) have been established in collaboration with thirty-eight SSCs.[34] Similarly, through the Pradhan Mantri Kaushal Vikas Yojana (PMKVY), a flagship skill development scheme of the government, three million candidates have been trained and one million placed with the support of 2,250 training partners.[35]

A skill development programme, structured with a deep understanding of the industry's talent requirements, allows for a demand-driven approach towards reshaping the higher education–training–employment value chain—thus allowing for training programmes to provide relevant technical skills. There is also a strong move to embed soft skills training modules and sessions on workforce readiness as a part of skill development courses, as it reduces workplace attrition and increases the potential for career progression. Apart from soft skills, employers cited lack of workplace readiness in terms of poor résumés, inability to showcase skills sets, under par communication skills and lack of understanding of the industry or the workplace as the main reasons for not extending employment, or for workplace-attrition.[36] The NSDC's report on the impact of its skill development initiatives highlights the limited uptake of apprenticeships by the youth and the high attrition observed both during the course and post-placement.[37] The gap demonstrates the need to include a workforce readiness module in the delivery of current training programmes to enhance employability.

Figure 3 maps challenges identified by the MSDE that prevail in the Indian skilling ecosystem. A set of potential intervention pathways linked to the four skill categories in line with 4IR have been outlined.

The four skill categories can provide the right foundation for the youth to emerge as an engaged workforce, gaining industry-specific skill-sets while setting a pathway towards lifelong learning. The potential remains for the government to emerge as a centralizing catalyst to structure hybrid skilling programmes focused on 4IR through collaborative initiatives with business, not-for-profits and individuals.

WHO SHOULD PREPARE THE INDIAN YOUTH FOR 4IR?

The vocational training ecosystem in India is oriented towards addressing the widening skills gap in order to meet industrial requirements. There are multiple stakeholders and models of skill development that have evolved over the last ten years such as school-linked vocational training, university-embedded initiatives, apprenticeship approaches, public-private partnerships (PPPs) and enterprise development-focused programmes. Collaboration and coordination across a range of stakeholders will support the success of the youth. Some of the key challenges that stakeholders should keep in perspective are:

- How to reimagine 4IR as a unique opportunity instead of a problem?
- How to reposition approaches at a unified, platform level?
- How to align, to achieve both scale and impact?
- How to reframe the possibilities in 4IR for marginalized youth?[38]

The skill development compass presented in Figure 4 places the intended audience—the youth—at the centre. The compass indicates various pathways of accessing skill-sets required to succeed in the era of 4IR. Currently, the youth can access a skill development course at a higher education institute, university, industrial training institutes (ITIs), corporate foundation-linked vocational training centres, not-for-profits or an NSDC-aligned centre.

Potential Areas of Intervention

Improving workforce readiness
Workforce readiness is necessary for entry into—and ongoing success in—the workplace. It ranges from the initial job search to maintaining continuous employment.

Areas of intervention:
- Supporting youth in finding and securing appropriate employment
- Enabling them to succeed within their workplace by equipping them with up-to-date curriculum and pedagogy
- Supporting skill development programmes that develop literacy, numeracy, digital literacy, resume writing, time management and professionalism, among other skills
- Industry exposure

Improving soft skills
Soft skills are personal attributes—social and communication skills that support interpersonal relationship development.

Areas of intervention:
- Supporting programmes which enable candidates to better adapt with internal and external stakeholders at their workplace
- Supporting skill development programmes which stress on improving communication, collaboration, adaptability, teamwork and self-confidence

Improving technical skills
Technical skills are the knowledge and capabilities required to perform specialized tasks.

Areas of intervention:
- Supporting skill development programmes which give the youth the technical and domain expertise needed to perform job-specific tasks with pre-qualification exposure visits and practicums
- Supporting skill development programmes that include sessions on computer programming, coding, project management, financial management and mechanical functions

Supporting entrepreneurship
Entrepreneurial skills are the knowledge and abilities that support creating and building a workplace.

Areas of intervention:
- Supporting youth in understanding entrepreneurial models and establishing their own businesses
- Supporting skill development programmes which include sessions on innovation, creativity, resourcefulness, risk-taking and business acumen

Figure 3

Source: *Derived from the Four Skill Categories in Deloitte, Preparing Tomorrow's Workforce for the Fourth Industrial Revolution, September 2018*

SUBHA SRINIVASAN AND KUMAR KANDASWAMI ↦

The vocational training ecosystem in India is oriented towards addressing the widening skills gap in order to meet industrial requirements.

A hybrid implementation approach—depicted through the compass—enables the youth to access skill training programmes across varied pathways, maximizing impact and returns on investments. At each stage, leveraging industry tie-ups signifies the role of business. Industry has provided significant support through corporate social responsibility (CSR) funding in establishing skill training centres, strengthening set-ups within government-linked ITIs and funding NGO-driven vocational training models. However, a gap remains in bringing industrial know-how to the delivery of training courses. Business has a key role in defining the skills required, establishing standards for training and certification, credentialing youth coming from technical schools in the formal sector and providing opportunities to grow further through broadened understanding or experiential learning. The business community should recognize that a skill-driven approach to reshape job roles and contexts can support youth to grow at the workplace.[39]

As the government system and public authorities prepare for 4IR, higher levels of efficiency are called for, and agility and collaboration with business and civil society are necessitated. The government is a critical catalyst between stakeholders in the education system—employers and the youth. It has the ability to maximize impact by leveraging its size and resources to strengthen the skilling ecosystem. In addition, skill development initiatives, linked with government-defined training standards or certifications, facilitates credentialing and enhancing the market value of the training candidates. Engaging the not-for-profit sector in mobilization, counselling youth and their families, and providing training is equally critical in reinforcing the skilling value chain.

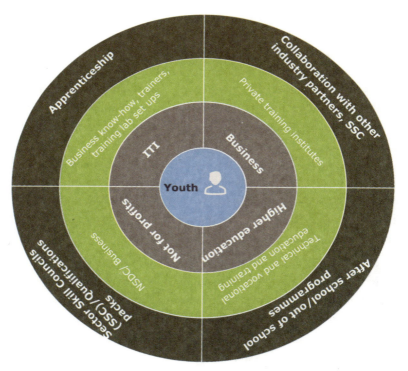

Figure 4: Skill Compass: Demand-driven collaborative skill training ecosystem models led by government, business and not-for-profits

A benefit of the hybrid skill development models—including PPPs—designed in consultation or collaboration with business, is the introduction of state-of-the-art training infrastructure or technology labs to meet industry requirements. It is a winning combination brought together by a set of invested stakeholders, each contributing their technical expertise, community rapport and industry linkages and ensuring training quality based on set standards. Youth are trained across batches for specific sets of employers with funding from both business and soft loans from government-affiliated entities like the NSDC. Conversely, the limitations in such demand-driven models include continuity in funding, shifts in technology and industry requirement. Some of these limitations can be perceived as opportunities by the government to engage industry further in designing collaborative initiatives, with added avenues for funding and knowledge on industry trends.

THE WAY AHEAD

Building on the earlier section, which delineates the role of various stakeholders in the skilling ecosystem, suggestions on collaboration, the nature of work across the three economies and gender-specific programme concepts are outlined below.

1. Collaboration

The government, business and communities should adopt a collaborative approach through a platform to meet the requirements of Industry 4.0 and address the skill gaps in creating 8.1 million jobs annually. Such an initiative at scale will limit duplication of efforts and allow invested stakeholders to maximize impact across the education spectrum in the following ways:

    a.   Improving the quality of higher education, technical and non-technical.

b. Shifting parameters of success for educational attainment (skill-based economy).
c. Upgrading core competitiveness of vocational training schools.
d. Strengthening recruitment and training of talent through in-house skills training set-ups.
e. Enabling opportunities for entrepreneurship.

2. Workforce across the three economies

The Deloitte report on 'Preparing Tomorrow's Workforce for the 4IR' highlights the advantages of the 'three economies' approach in developing countries, where a significant section of the population is employed in the informal sector and located in remote areas.[40] It allows workers to build, adapt and grow with a set of skills flowing from the informal gigs to formal economies.[41] A triangulated flow of skills provides opportunities for skill building, training and apprenticeships and enterprise development to youth with limited resources and access, raising their chances of social mobility.

3. Gender focus

The declining female labour force participation in India highlights the need for gendered initiatives to improve women's participation in the workforce.[42] Women continue to face numerous socio-economic-cultural barriers that limit their labour force participation. Interestingly, as the nature of work shifts with constructs like the unleashed workforce and emergence of adhocracy organizations, women with relevant skill sets will have improved opportunities for further flexibility and inclusion.[43] Women in rural areas express a willingness to work if the employment is local. This demonstrates the potential for local-level scaling of enterprise development initiatives for women such as those introduced by Mann Deshi or Development Alternatives,[44]—the programmes that have continued to display outcomes like economic empowerment, social inclusion and increased agency. In developing economies, the World Bank has structured intervention concepts like safe transport, flexible schedules and childcare support for women, largely from rural and semi-urban areas, that are enrolled in vocational training courses to improve chances of continuity and potential to take up employment.[45]

> The business community recognizing how a skill-driven approach, can reshape job roles and contexts can support youth to grow at the workplace.

CREATING VALUE TOGETHER

4IR is an ongoing phenomenon with exponentially increasing reach. Government, business and community are all well positioned to gain from the opportunity, recognize the challenges and prepare our youth for the future of work. It presents a great platform for collaboration, innovation, entrepreneurship and solutions to some of society's pressing issues. 4IR has the potential to improve global income levels, reduce inequalities and improve quality of life through a range of technological innovations. As Schwab highlights, 'It comes down to people and values, where the future of work puts people first and empowers them.'[46]

REFERENCES

1. The authors gratefully acknowledge the contribution of Timothy Hanley, Global Leader, Industrial Products and Construction, Deloitte, and Mark Cotteleer, Research Director, Centre for Integrated Research, Deloitte, USA.
2. International Monetary Fund. India Country Report, No 18/254.
3. Ibid.
4. Ibid.
5. World Bank Group 'Labour force participation rate'. https://data.worldbank.org/indicator/SL.TLF.CACT.ZS
6. Economic Survey 2018.
7. Ministry of Women and Child Development. 'Study of Working Women and Privileges in the Unorganized Sector'. 2016. http://www.wcd.nic.in/sites/default/files/FINAL%20DRAFT%20REPORT_0.pdf
8. International Monetary Fund. Pursuing Women's Economic Empowerment, May 2018
9. Government of India, Ministry of Skill Development & Entrepreneurship. National Skill Development Mission. https://www.msde.gov.in/assets/images/Mission%20booklet.pdf
10. Klaus Schwab, 'The fourth industrial revolution', https://www.weforum.org/about/the-fourth-industrial-revolution-by-klaus-schwab, accessed on 22 December 2018
11. Deloitte, *The Evolution of Work*. 2018.
12. ibid
13. Deloitte. 'The fourth industrial revolution is here – are you ready?', 2018.
14. Deloitte, *The Evolution of Work*. 2018.
15. Daniel Pink, 'A Whole New Mind', 2006, https://vision4learning.wordpress.com/current-reading/daniel-pink-a-whole-new-mind/.
16. International Labour Organization, 'Attracting Skilled International Migrants to China', 2017, https://www.ilo.org/wcmsp5/groups/

public/---asia/---ro-bangkok/---ilo-beijing/documents/publication/wcms_565474.pdf.
17. All India Status of Education Report. 2017, Beyond Basics. http://img.asercentre.org/docs/Publications/ASER%20Reports/ASER%202017/aser2017fullreportfinal.pdf
18. Government of India, Ministry of Labour and Employment, March 2018, http://labourbureaunew.gov.in/QES_7th_round_Report_final_12032018.pdf, accessed on 24 December 2018
19. 'China's skilled workers incentivized to succeed', 24-3-2018, http://www.xinhuanet.com/english/2018-03/24/c_137061740.htm
20. 'Only 6 out of those passing out of Engineering colleges are fit for a job', 4-June-2018, https://economictimes.indiatimes.com/jobs/only-6-of-those-passing-out-of-indias-engineering-colleges-are-fit-for-a-job/articleshow/64446292.cms
21. Aspiring Minds, National Employability Report, 2016, https://www.aspiringminds.com/sites/default/files/National%20Employability%20Report%20-%20Engineers%20Annual%20Report%202016.pdf
22. Deloitte, 'Preparing Tomorrow's Workforce for the Fourth Industrial Revolution', September 2018
23. The Education Commission. 'The international finance facility for Education', p.2, http://educationcommission.org/wp-content/uploads/2018/05/EC_IFFEd_Prospectus-1.pdf, accessed on 22 December 18
24. Deloitte, 'Preparing Tomorrow's Workforce for the Fourth Industrial Revolution', September 2018
25. International Labour Organisation, 'The World Employment and Social Outlook Trends', 2018, https://www.ilo.org/wcmsp5/groups/public/---dgreports/---dcomm/---publ/documents/publication/wcms_615594.pdf, accessed on 28 December 2018
26. Economic Survey 2018, Indian Labour Market, NSSO
27. Government of India, Ministry of Labour and Employment, March 2018, http://labourbureaunew.gov.in/QES_7th_round_Report_final_12032018.pdf, accessed on 24 December 2018
28. Ministry of Skill Development and Entrepreneurship, Annual Report, 2016-17, https://www.msde.gov.in/assets/images/annual%20report/

Annual%20Report%202016-2017%20-%20English.pdf
29. Observer Research Foundation, 'Young India and Work', 2018, https://www.orfonline.org/research/young-india-and-work-a-survey-of-youth-aspirations-45455/, accessed on 28 December 2018
30. The Sustainable Development Goals (SDGs), introduced by the United Nations are a set of Global Goals to end poverty, protect the planet and ensure that all people enjoy peace and prosperity. These seventeen Goals build on the successes of the Millennium Development Goals. http://www.undp.org/content/undp/en/home/sustainable-development-goals.html
31. PRS, The apprentices amendment bill, 2014, http://www.prsindia.org/uploads/media/Apprentices%20(A)/Apprentices%20(A)%20bill,%202014.pdf
32. Deloitte, 'Preparing Tomorrow's Workforce for the Fourth Industrial Revolution', September 2018
33. Not-for-profit, social enterprises, Section 25 companies, etc.
34. ational Skill Development Corporation, https://www.nsdcindia.org/partners.
35. PMKVY. http://pmkvyofficial.org/Dashboard.aspx
36. Deloitte, 'NSDC Impact Assessment Report', 2016
37. Chenoy, Dilip, 'Aligning Skills with Jobs', *Journal of Development Policy and Practice*. 2017.
38. Derived from Deloitte, 'Preparing Tomorrow's Workforce for the Fourth Industrial Revolution', September 2018
39. Deloitte, 'Preparing Tomorrow's Workforce for the Fourth Industrial Revolution', September 2018
40. ibid
41. Gig economy is a blending of formal and informal economies.
42. International Labour Organisation, 'Women's Labour Force Participation in India –why is it so low?' , https://www.ilo.org/wcmsp5/groups/public/---asia/---ro-bangkok/---sro-new_delhi/documents/genericdocument/wcms_342357.pdf
43. Adhocracy refers to flexible, adaptive and informal work structures which are aligned to realities such as the unleashed workforce and nimble enterprise.

44. Mann Deshi Foundation, http://manndeshifoundation.org/ and Development Alternatives, https://www.devalt.org/.
45. World Bank, Women in India's Economic Growth, 2018, https://www.worldbank.org/en/news/speech/2018/03/17/women-indias-economic-growth
46. Klaus Schwab, 'The fourth industrial revolution: what it means and how to respond', 2016, https://www.weforum.org/agenda/2016/01/the-fourth-industrial-revolution-what-it-means-and-how-to-respond/

CONTRIBUTORS

Fatih Birol has served as Executive Director of the International Energy Agency (IEA) since September 2015. Under his leadership, the IEA has undertaken its first comprehensive modernization programme since the creation of the Agency in 1974. Prior to his nomination as Executive Director, Dr Birol spent twenty years as a staff member at the Agency, serving most recently as Chief Economist. He has been named as one of the most influential people on the world's energy scene by Forbes and was recognized by the *Financial Times* as energy personality of the year in 2017. He is the Founder and Chair of the IEA Energy Business Council, one of the most active industry advisory groups in global energy. He also chairs the World Economic Forum's (Davos) Energy Advisory Board and serves on the UN Secretary-General's Advisory Board on 'Sustainable Energy for All'.

Daniel Yergin is a highly respected authority on energy, international politics and economics. He was awarded the Pulitzer Prize for his book, *The Prize: The Epic Quest for Oil, Money and Power.*

Time Magazine said, 'If there is one man whose opinion matters more than any other on global energy markets, it's Daniel Yergin.' *Fortune* said that he is 'one of the planet's foremost thinkers about energy and its implications.' *The New York Times* described Daniel Yergin as 'America's most influential energy pundit'.

He is Vice Chairman of IHS and Founder of IHS Cambridge Energy Research Associates. He also serves on the US Secretary of Energy's Advisory Board and chaired the US Department of Energy's Task Force on Strategic Energy Research and Development. The Prime Minister of India presented Daniel Yergin with a Lifetime Achievement Award in 2014. The same year the US Department of Energy awarded him the first James Schlesinger Medal for Energy Security.

Anil Kakodkar obtained his BE Hons degree from Bombay University in 1963 and MSc from Nottingham University in 1969. He joined the Bhabha Atomic Research Centre (BARC) in 1964 and became its Director in 1996. He was Chairman of the Atomic Energy Commission and Secretary to the Government of India, Department of Atomic Energy, during 2000–09. India's atomic energy programme received a significant boost through the contributions and leadership of Dr Kakodkar. He conceptualized and built Dhruva, one of the largest research reactors, and was among the key individuals responsible for the nuclear explosion experiment in 1974 and the nuclear weapons tests in 1998. He also pioneered indigenous development of a pressurized heavy water power reactor system and the design of a Thorium-powered advanced heavy water reactor. He has been felicitated with all the three Padma awards, besides numerous others. He presently devotes his time to issues related to energy, education and knowledge-enabled rural development.

Mohammad Sanusi Barkindo began his tenure as Secretary General of OPEC on 1 August 2016. Over the years he has also worked in several other key roles at OPEC. From 2009 to 2010, he was Group Managing Director and CEO of the Nigerian National Petroleum Corporation (NNPC). Prior to that, he served as Deputy Managing Director of Nigerian Liquefied Natural Gas. He has also been leader of Nigeria's technical delegation to the UN climate change negotiations since 1991. He served as Chair of the Group of 77 and China at the United Nations Framework Convention on Climate Change (UNFCCC) and was elected to serve three terms as Vice President of the Conference of the Parties—CoP13 (Bali), CoP14 (Poznan) and

CoP15 (Copenhagen), where he chaired the opening session. Since becoming Secretary General, he has been a leading voice in the long quest for more OPEC and non-OPEC cooperation for stable oil markets on a sustainable basis.

Kirk R. Smith, MPH, Phd, is Professor of Global Environmental Health at the University of California, Berkeley, and Director of the Collaborative Clean Air Policy Centre, New Delhi. He has done research on household fuel issues in India since 1978, including conducting the first measurements of household air pollution in the world—in Gujarat in 1981. With colleagues and students, he has done fieldwork in more than a dozen Indian states as well as Nepal, China, Guatemala, Mongolia, Mexico and Laos, and investigated a range of health outcomes from these exposures. He is also active in climate research and was the co-leader of the health chapter of the last assessment of the Intergovernmental Panel on Climate Change (IPCC), sharing the 2007 Nobel Peace Prize with the IPCC team. He is a recipient of a number of international scientific awards in environment and is a member of the US National Academy of Sciences.

CONTRIBUTORS

Abhishek Jain is a Senior Programme Lead at the Council on Energy, Environment and Water (CEEW). He heads the Council's research on energy access. With more than eight years of experience, Abhishek has worked on multiple issues at the confluence of energy, economics, environment and policy. His research (and action) spans energy provision and use for households, communities, and livelihoods. He co-conceptualized—and leads—CEEW's flagship research efforts on Access to Clean Cooking energy and Electricity–Survey of States (ACCESS), the largest survey of its kind on energy access. Over the years, Abhishek has focused on various issues including renewable energy, decentralized energy access, clean cooking energy, liquefied petroleum gas (LPG) for cooking, fossil fuel subsidies, electricity sector reforms, solar-powered irrigation and circular economy. He holds an MPhil from the University of Cambridge and a BTech from IIT Roorkee.

Dharmendra Pradhan is the Union Minister for Petroleum and Natural Gas and Skill Development and Entrepreneurship in the Government of India. He has spearheaded many progressive reforms and initiatives to empower rural India with the clean fuel—LPG—under the aegis of the immensely popular Pradhan Mantri Ujjwala Yojana under which eighty million LPG connections are being provided to women from below poverty line (BPL) families by 2022. He is also attributed with several successful consumer initiatives like PAHAL, which is the world's largest direct benefit transfer scheme, and the #GiveItUp campaign, which saw ten million affluent citizens surrender their LPG subsidy for those who need it.

A postgraduate in anthropology from Utkal University, Bhubaneswar, he has been working on several issues concerning the youth and the rehabilitation and resettlement of farmers. After taking charge as Skill Development and Entrepreneurship Minister, he has been focusing on reskilling and skilling India's manpower, and bridging the skill gap of India's youth.

Adil Zainulbhai is Chairman of the Quality Council of India. An alumni of IIT Bombay and Harvard Business School, he is currently the president of the Harvard Business School's alumni association in India. He is the former chairman of McKinsey India. Apart from counselling the CEOs of many of India's largest companies, he also works closely with the government to drive growth, strengthen key sectors of the economy and improve education, health and welfare. He speaks regularly at key forums, including those of the Confederation of Indian Industry (CII), the Federation of Indian Chambers of Commerce and Industry, the National Association of Software and Services Companies (NASSCOM) and the World Economic Forum. He also serves

CONTRIBUTORS ▸

on the advisory boards of IIT-Bombay, the Wockhardt Foundation and the Health Management Research Institute, as well as on the global advisory board of the University of Chicago's Booth School of Business.

Arvind Panagariya is Professor of Economics and Jagdish Bhagwati Professor of Indian Political Economy at Columbia University. During 2015–17, he served as the first Vice Chairman of NITI Aayog, Government of India, in the rank of a cabinet minister. In that time, he served as India's G20 Sherpa and led the teams that negotiated the G20 Communiqués during presidencies of Turkey (2015), China (2016) and Germany (2017). He is a former Chief Economist of the Asian Development Bank and was on the faculty of the Department of Economics at the University of Maryland at College Park (1978–2003). During these years, he also worked with the World Bank, International Monetary Fund (IMF) and United Nations Conference on Trade and Development (UNCTAD) in various capacities.

Professor Panagariya has authored more than fifteen books. Scientific papers by him have appeared in top journals such as the *American Economic Review* and *Quarterly Journal of Economics* while policy papers by him have appeared in *Foreign Affairs* and *Foreign Policy*, alongside columns in various newspapers. In March 2012, the Government of India awarded Professor Panagariya the Padma Bhushan, the third highest civilian honour in the country.

Anil Kumar Jain is a member of the Indian Administrative Service of the Government of India and is presently posted as Additional Secretary in the Ministry of Environment, Forest and Climate Change, handling issues related to environmental clearances, hazardous substances and wetlands, among other things. He has over three decades of administrative experience at the field and policy formulation levels and has held senior positions in the central and state governments in multiple ministries, including Petroleum and Natural Gas—an area in which he specializes. He led India's delegation to the Energy and Climate Working Group of G20 for five years (2012–17). During that time, as Head of the Energy Division of the National Institution for Transforming India, he led several integrated modelling initiatives, including the India Energy Security Scenarios, 2047 (IESS). He also led the team that drafted the National Energy Policy (2017–40). He has authored the book *Natural Gas in India: Policy and Liberalisation* and publishes articles in various journals, including *Energy Policy*.

Debasish Mishra leads the energy, resources and industrial products industry for Deloitte Touche Tohmatsu in India. He is a Partner in the consulting function of Deloitte with more than two decades of experience in the energy sector in India and several other developed and developing countries.

CONTRIBUTORS ▸▸

Debasish has been advising governments, sector regulators, energy companies, investors and multilateral agencies in a range of issues in various sectors. He has been a keen observer and contributor to India's energy policy as it transitions towards a low carbon future.

Satya S. Tripathi is UN Assistant Secretary General and Head of New York Office at UN Environment. A development economist and lawyer with over thirty-five years of varied experience, he has served with the UN since 1998 in key positions in Europe, Asia and Africa in the areas of climate change, human rights, democratic governance and legal affairs. Among other crucial positions, he was Executive Head of UNORCID—established by the UN Secretary General in 2011 to facilitate a US $1 billion REDD+ partnership between Indonesia, Norway and other stakeholders on climate change mitigation through the conservation of forests and preservation of peatland and biodiversity.

Tripathi is a Senior Distinguished Fellow on Natural Resources Governance at the World Agroforestry Centre (ICRAF) and serves on the Advisory Council of the Natural Capital Declaration (NCD). He previously served on the World Economic Forum's Global Advisory Council on Forests; and in India as a member of its National Civil Service.

S. Jaishankar is President—Global Corporate Affairs at Tata Sons Limited from May 2018.

In that role, he is responsible for the Group's global corporate affairs and international strategy development. The international offices of Tata Sons across the world report to him. He works with Tata companies to help them to strengthen their business presence and positioning in geographies globally.

Earlier, Dr Jaishankar was Foreign Secretary from 2015–18, Ambassador to the United States from 2013–15, Ambassador to China from 2009–2013, High Commissioner to Singapore from 2007–2009 and Ambassador to the Czech Republic from 2000–2004.

He has also served in other diplomatic assignments in Embassies across Moscow, Colombo, Budapest and Tokyo, as well in the Ministry of External Affairs and the President's Secretariat.

Dr Jaishankar is a graduate of St. Stephen's College, University of Delhi. He has an MA in Political Science and an MPhil and PhD in International Relations from Jawaharlal Nehru University, Delhi.

Bob Dudley is BP's Group Chief Executive. He joined Amoco Corporation in 1979, working in a variety of engineering and commercial posts. In 1997 he became General Manager for Strategy for Amoco and in 1999, following the merger of BP and Amoco, was appointed to a similar role in BP. Between 1999 and 2000 he was Executive Assistant to the Group Chief Executive, subsequently becoming Group Vice President for BP's renewables and alternative energy activities. In 2002 he became Group Vice President responsible for BP's upstream businesses in Russia, the Caspian region, Angola, Algeria and Egypt. From 2003 to 2008 he was President and CEO of TNK-BP. On his return to BP in 2009, he was appointed to the BP board and oversaw the group's activities in the Americas and Asia. Between 23 June and 30 September 2010, he served as the President and CEO of BP's Gulf Coast Restoration Organization in the US. He was appointed a Director of Rosneft in March 2013 following BP's acquisition of a stake in Rosneft.

Nisha Biswal is President of the US–India Business Council (USIBC) at the US Chamber of Commerce. She provides strategic guidance and leads advocacy efforts on behalf of the USIBC's 300-odd member companies, promoting long-term commercial partnerships to advance the bilateral trade relationship between the US and India. She served as the assistant secretary for South and Central Asian Affairs at the US Department of State from 2013 to 2017. She was awarded the prestigious Samman Award by the President of India.

Prior to this, Biswal supervised USAID's activities across South and Southeast Asia, and spent over a decade in Capitol Hill. Most recently, Biswal served as a Senior Adviser at the Albright

Stonebridge Group. Biswal served on the board of the US Global Leadership Coalition and is a member of the US Institute of Peace International Advisory Council and the Institute for Sustainable Communities board of directors.

Ashwin Jacob is a Partner working with Deloitte Touché Tohmatsu India LLP in its Mumbai office. He has more than nineteen years of experience in the oil and gas and industrial sectors in India and several other countries. He currently leads the oil, gas and chemicals sector for Deloitte in India. Ashwin specializes in leading large complex multidisciplinary engagements which help clients achieve tangible short- and long-term goals through digital and organizational capability building initiatives. He has led over a hundred engagements, where he has worked closely with CxOs from Indian promoters, MNCs and large public sector enterprises on interventions spanning strategy formulation and implementation, organization design, supply chain and manufacturing optimization, technology strategy and customer and channel strategy design. Ashwin is a Mechanical Engineer from MS University, Baroda and an MBA in Strategy and Operations from the National Institute of Industrial Engineering (NITIE), Mumbai.

Shubha Srinivasan is a Director, Deloitte Touche Tohmatsu India LLP. She anchors the social impact practice for Deloitte, India, and has extensive experience in the development sector, corporate social responsibility (CSR) and public policy. She provides services for a wide range of companies, aid agencies, global foundations, and central and state governments in the development sector across areas like education, health and skill development. Shubha has also served as an Independent Director on the board of companies. Currently, she is a part of the AmCham CSR committee and CII's Western region CSR committee. She has a bachelor's degree from the University of Pennsylvania and an MSc in Public Policy and Management from SOAS, University of London.

Kumar Kandaswami is a Partner in Deloitte Touche Tohmatsu India LLP. He has over thirty years of consulting experience. He is Industries Practice Leader for Deloitte, India. In addition, he leads the industrial products and construction sector. He has published several research reports on the manufacturing and automotive sectors. In Deloitte, he has led the global manufacturing nerve centre, a research unit, been a member of the global manufacturing executive and chaired the Asia-Pacific manufacturing industry leadership board. In the areas of strategy and operations, he has served client organizations from diverse manufacturing sectors such as automotive, process chemicals, industrial goods and consumer products. Kumar is a member of the national manufacturing committee of Federation of Indian Chambers of Commerce & Industry (FICCI). He chairs the AmCham committee for supply chain and logistics, and the ET India leadership council for manufacturing. Kumar speaks frequently in academic and industry forums.